JOURNEYING WITH PAIN

FINDING HOPE WHEN YOU DON'T FIND ANSWERS

ALAN SEABORN

Copyright © 2018 Alan Seaborn. All rights reserved.

Published by Winning At Home, Zeeland, Michigan;

www.winningathome.com.

ISBN: 978-0-692-99425-2

All Scripture quotations are taken from the Holy Bible, New International Version®, NIV® Copyright ©1973, 1978, 1984, 2011 by Biblica, Inc.® Used by permission. All rights reserved worldwide.

Cover design by Navigate Creative Works.

Interior design by Navigate Creative Works.

For Annaliese:

Thanks for your prayers, strength, feedback, love, and challenges along the way. I look forward to seeing where this journey of ours takes us!

Thanks to my family and friends, who have been there for me as I've sought resolution. Thanks for your prayers and encouragement. And thanks to Dan and Jane (Dad and Mom), Jeff, Gregg, Steven, Dan, and Annaliese for reading through the drafts of this book and giving me much-needed feedback along the way!

Table of Contents

Introduction: *Getting There—Defining the Grief Journey of Pain* — *9*

Chapter 1: *Our First Response* — *19*

Chapter 2: *Denial* — *33*

Chapter 3: *Anger* — *49*

Chapter 4: *The Why of Suffering and Pain* — *65*

Chapter 5: *Bargaining* — *79*

Chapter 6: *Depression* — *97*

Chapter 7: *Acceptance* — *121*

Chapter 8: *Staying There* — *145*

NOTES — *153*

INTRODUCTION:

Getting There—Defining the Grief Journey of Pain

This book is for anyone in any kind of ongoing pain.

I never thought I'd be writing about pain in its role as a great teacher, and I'm probably one of the more reluctant carriers of this message. Even more than that, I never *wanted* what I'm writing about to be true. But as I tried to find helpful and encouraging resources while I was dealing with pain in my own life, I became open to writing about it. I'd found resources that touched on my situation in some ways that connected with me, but I'd never found that book or sermon or article or podcast that hit the sweet spot for me.

Throughout my journey I revisited this powerful C. S. Lewis reminder: "God whispers to us in our pleasures, speaks in our conscience, but shouts in our pain: it is His megaphone to rouse a deaf world."[1] I wish this weren't true, but I've found it to be the case. As a result of my pain, I have been opened to God's leading in a way I never imagined possible. It took about five years of living in constant turmoil before I finally surrendered and let him start leading, but I eventually got there.

In the chapters to come, I lay out my journey and approach what I've learned in three ways:

Understanding the Stages of Grief as Experienced through Pain

First, it may have seemed obvious to everybody else, but as I was going through this roller coaster, I never realized how closely my emotional state resembled the stages of grief: anger, denial, bargaining, depression, and acceptance. The premise of this book is that these stages are normal, natural, and to be expected. However, that doesn't mean everything we do or think in each stage is healthy. Using my own journey as the path, we'll look at how I personally experienced each of these stages of grief. Perhaps you'll recognize one or more stages of your own journey.

Biblical Heroes Struggled Too

Second, we'll look at how some people in the Bible mishandled each of these stages. I've often heard people dealing with pain and suffering encouraged to see if anybody in the Bible dealt with a similar challenge. That's a great first instinct, because it allows us to learn from the experience and wisdom of others instead of basing decisions solely on our own experience. The biblical examples we'll review will help us see we're not alone, recognize how common it is to respond in an unhealthy way, and offer some instructive guardrails we can put in place as we deal with similar emotions. I want to help us see that even if we feel that our emotional responses are disproportionate to the pain or loss or disappointment in our lives, it's natural to experience this grief cycle.

Where possible, we'll focus on biblical characters who are positive, admirable examples in dealing with these emotions. But, as I said, we'll also look at how otherwise godly people responded in unhealthy ways to some of these emotions. Some of the examples may make you feel that I'm stretching the definition of grief a bit, but I want to show that these emotions come along with everything from pain, suffering, and loss to disappointment, unmet expectations, and failure.

Imitating the Way of Jesus

Third, we'll look at how Jesus, too, handled these challenges, with the goal of basing our responses on his life. Writing in *The Power of Parable* on looking to Jesus as the role model for dealing with the array of emotions that emerge from pain and suffering, John Dominic Crossan pointed out why it's so important that Jesus successfully navigated this difficult journey: "If it were done, it could be done again—and by others. That, of course, is the challenge of Jesus as an actual, factual, historical figure. If any one human being can do anything in life and death, other human beings can do likewise."[2] What Jesus modeled is an example all of us dealing with pain and suffering would do well to emulate.

My Journey with Pain—the Backstory

In the summer of 2011, I was a groomsman in a wedding when I started feeling lightheaded and woozy during the ceremony. I'm a public speaker, so I'm comfortable in front of people and I wasn't nervous. I also knew I hadn't locked my knees or anything like that, and I hadn't had any alcohol to drink. I grabbed on to my brother's shoulder (he was the groomsman right in front of me) to stabilize myself for the rest of the ceremony. I think knowing the other guys with me in the wedding would never let me hear the end of it if I passed out was the main thing that kept me standing!

I wasn't worried at this point. My plan was to just make it through the wedding ceremony and figure out what was going on with me later. When I got to the reception, however, I realized the feeling still hadn't gone away. And

Introduction

then I woke up feeling the same way the next morning. As days turned into weeks, I tried to explain what I was experiencing to the people in my life. I called it a weird mixture of dizziness, brain fog, spacey-ness, and fatigue.

More than six years later, I still feel that way from the time I wake up in the morning until the time I go to sleep at night. I never experience relief. I never have "good" days when I feel normal, and some days I feel even worse.

I finally figured out the best way to describe how I always feel: like I slept for only one hour the night before. When I really don't get enough sleep, the only difference is that I have a headache in addition to everything else.

I've never fallen or lost consciousness, but I've had sudden woozy spells, and I've seen my vision slowly go black as the tunnel closed in. I've grown accustomed to all this, but I'm sure people around me are surprised when I bend over with my hands on my knees to gather myself or lean against a wall or doorframe for stability.

When this whole journey started, I was more annoyed than worried. I thought I'd be able to get to the bottom of my problem quickly with a few visits to the doctor and some tests. Even if this was a worst-case scenario, I'd seen the TV show *House*. I believed if my condition escalated and I deteriorated over time, someone would eventually figure out what was wrong before I died from some weird, unknown thing.

However, my experience has been quite different. I've seen allergists, sleep specialists, ENTs, neurologists, functional medicine doctors, rheumatologists, acupuncturists, and dieticians. I've had MRIs, x-rays, EKGs, ultrasounds, and an obscene amount of blood work done. Just about every one of these appointments started the same way: the doctors and specialists told me they saw this type of thing often and they'd have me feeling better in a couple of weeks. And then every one of those doctors and specialists ended up saying they couldn't find anything wrong with me. Any of you dealing with a chronic or undiagnosed health issue know how emotionally draining this cycle can be.

For about six months, I took an optimistic approach to what I was facing. I still felt like it was simply a matter of finding the right doctor. The only real issue I was worried about was how much money I was spending trying to figure out which doctor was the right one. I hated how I was feeling, but this experience felt like a strange side story to my life rather than the main storyline. As time wore on, though, I started to feel like my condition was becoming more and more of the central storyline of my life.

That's the big-picture backstory for what eventually brought me to the point of writing this book. I fully recognize some people have suffered unimaginably more than I have. Those of you who have experienced abuse of any kind, the loss of a loved one, a debilitating injury or condition, or any number of physical or mental struggles might read about my journey and be tempted to think, *Wow, I'd trade places with that guy in a second.* I know, because I've had the same thought!

There can be a sick component to dealing with pain. When you're in the middle of it, it has an almost blinding effect. In *The Meaning of Marriage*, Timothy and Kathy Keller write, "We are always, always the last to see our self-absorption. Our hurts and wounds can make our self-centeredness even more intractable. When you point out selfish behavior to a wounded person, he or she will say, 'Well, maybe so, but you don't understand what it is like.' The wounds justify the behavior."[3]

I've since had a perspective change, but I can absolutely vouch for the truth of that claim. In the first few years of dealing with my symptoms, I found myself completely unable to empathize with anybody whose pain I considered significantly less than my own. Just speaking for myself, that made me a worse person. I'm competitive by nature, so I guess it's only natural that I found myself "winning" when it came to comparing my suffering to that of others. What a small way to view the world!

As I've examined my own inner monologue, I've realized how sick that response was. Regardless of whether a person's pain and suffering is greater or lesser than somebody else's, the experience of being in pain or dealing with suffering is awful, no matter how significant—or not—the pain or suffering may be. Once I realized this, it wasn't too difficult to make the leap to understanding that, on some level, we're all in this together. Even if our own "suffering" is at a lower level, we all know the feeling of being unable to accomplish what we want to accomplish. We all know the feeling of being denied an opportunity we'd been looking forward to. We all know what it feels like to be on the sidelines, watching helplessly as a tragedy on any level unfolds right in front of us.

I like to discuss nuance, so writing a book has been particularly challenging for me. I find myself having to imagine responses or criticisms people may have and then trying to answer that imagined feedback. So here's my big disclaimer: I am not writing about pain as an expert. I am not writing about pain as somebody who has experienced some unimaginable form of pain. I do not find any value in comparing and competing when it comes to "who suffered most." I simply want to share bits and pieces of my own personal journey, along with the lessons I've learned along the way.

I'm convinced that even though a quick fix would be preferable, the growth that takes place throughout this grief journey is unbelievably valuable. Only after I worked my way through these stages of grief did I realize what had been going on throughout that process. I was telling somebody about my failed visit to the Mayo Clinic after I'd come home without a diagnosis. "I expected to be devastated by this news," I said, "but instead I've accepted that I have to keep dealing with this." It wasn't until I heard myself say that word—*accepted*—that I realized I had been through these stages at all.

It took me more than five years to realize I was going through this cycle of the stages of grief. And I'm guessing many readers will see themselves in my story and personally identify with experiencing unexpected emotions at seemingly random times and with little provocation.

A Final Word as We Begin

I've done my best to remain completely honest and transparent in this book. And I don't want to sound like I've found some magical solution I'm trying to sell you. We've all heard people who've been through difficult times say, "I've grown so much. I wouldn't trade this experience for anything." I'm not one of those people. I know those others have a mature perspective, and I completely understand the point they're making, but that's not my mind-set yet. Maybe one day.

What I can tell you now, however, is that I *have* grown through this season of life, even as I'm making peace with the fact that this challenge may not end up being for just a season. I've learned so much about myself, and I've grown so much in my relationship with God, in my relationship with my wife, and in my ability to relate to other people in pain.

My hope and prayer is that others dealing with pain or suffering or grief can find encouragement as well as a challenge to grow in these pages. That's how I believe God works in our lives—he challenges and encourages us. My experience is that he usually does both at the same time.

CHAPTER 1

Our First Response

If pain is the great teacher, then I'm the reluctant student. Regardless, and as much as I wish it weren't true, I've learned from experience that pain and suffering present an opportunity for us to be transformed.

The biggest problem with this transformation is that we have the option to change in a positive way or a negative way. The most natural response to pain is to become bitter and angry and let our experience become our entire focus. But the longer we live this way, the more our world shrinks to a smaller and smaller size.

In addition, when we're less sympathetic toward the people around us with their minor (in our minds) concerns and complaints, they are more reluctant to share themselves with us. They know we won't lend a friendly ear to discuss life. And the longer we live this way—with this inward focus—the more damage we do to our relationships.

If instead we choose to deal with our pain in a positive way, we can get to a place of handing our frustrations and expectations to God rather than trying to carry them on our own. I'm guessing we've all gone down this path to some degree as we've experienced pain and suffering, and that we've asked *why* and *how* this could be happening. Those are valid questions. Where we can go wrong is focusing *only* on these questions. That's where I went wrong.

I am a rational, cause-and-effect sort of person, so I started out dealing with my undiagnosed health issue in a rational, cause-and-effect way. I thought back through all the unique experiences that could have caused my unique symptoms. I spent a year doing ministry in South Africa, so I analyzed that time. What had I potentially eaten, touched, inhaled, or otherwise been exposed to? I went through the same line of questioning for several short-term earthquake relief trips I'd taken to Haiti. I came up with some unique experiences and exposures, but when I talked with my doctors about them, they didn't seem to think they could be connected to how I was feeling.

Then I started thinking through other environmental and behavioral factors that may have caused my issues. I thought about the house I lived in with black mold that I didn't discover for a couple of years. I thought about the surgeries I had undergone. Was this a reaction to something used in the process of surgery or recovery? If so, why would it be hitting me with these symptoms years later? Could it be diet related? Something in the environment of my house or office?

I nearly drove myself crazy, and I have a feeling some of you can relate to that. There is nothing wrong with thinking through this line of questioning, but it can quickly devolve into obsession over every little thing and trying to pull everything into your control. Your world gets smaller because you want to expose yourself to fewer and fewer potential "contaminants"—whatever that word means to you at that point.

That approach generally leaves you self-centered and zoned in on your own needs and experiences. But considering and valuing others amid that pain doesn't mean forgetting about or minimizing your own pain. It means holding both truths in balance at the same time: *I am in pain and have specific needs as a result. But with effort, I can also see through and past my pain and appreciate the needs of others.*

If you're anything like me, that concept might be annoying. You don't want to be challenged to work on yourself *on top of everything else* you're already working through. It feels unfair. If I'm already doing so much emotional work to just keep my head above water, worrying about other people feels like an unbearable burden on top of the one I'm already carrying. But we must keep looking to our source of strength. Jesus shows us the better (and harder) way. The way of graciousness and forgiveness and generosity, even from the cross.

The Unhealthy Answer

The Buddhist worldview has what are called the Four Noble Truths. Truth number one is expressed in different ways, but my favorite translation is "life is suffering." Sometimes the wording is "suffering exists" or "the truth of suffering." I'm a big believer in the fact that all truth is God's truth, so I have no problem telling you about my admiration for snippets from other belief systems. The *first* thing Buddhists believe is that life is suffering. Let that sink in for a moment. They don't dance around reality and try to talk about the comfort we've all been denied, the comfort we deeply deserve. Buddhism is straight up in its honesty about the nature of reality—to be alive is to experience pain. That's part of the deal.

If I'm not careful, I can live in that idea a little bit too comfortably. It resonates a little too deeply sometimes. The cynical or nihilistic approach can be easier. If we learn we're *supposed* to be apathetic because we should expect only suffering, we can initially find freedom in that idea. It tells us to embrace the pain and suffering because everything is meaningless, and feeling something—even something bad—is better than feeling nothing. That's a sad place to live.

This response is distinct from experiencing some form of depression, because a motivation or justification is behind it. If we allow ourselves to think a bad situation can never change, then embracing nihilism is a way to feel as though we'll regain control over our circumstances. That's a big part of the reason it's so alluring. Nihilism allows us to explain and understand why our problems are going the way they are. If we can tell ourselves life is full of pain because that's exactly what we should expect to happen, we can take great comfort in that. We can *almost* embrace the moment because we're told that's what makes us truly alive.

This approach does have its merits. It can help us to accept our circumstances while putting much less effort into finding out the what, the why, and the how behind them. The issue, though, is that it's ultimately an empty philosophy. At the end of the line, we're left with no reason to hope for or to expect life to be any different in the future.

In his masterful work *The Gifts of the Jews*, Thomas Cahill outlines what I believe to be the origin of this belief.

He writes about the world that existed when God called Abram out of his land into a place God would show him. Cahill gives an overview of the worldview that dominated nearly every single culture on earth at the time. He explains how cultures from all over the world looked up at the heavens and saw the cycle of the moon waxing and waning and the predictability of the constellations; how those cultures looked at the earth and saw the cycle of the seasons and the birth, growth, peak, decline, and death of people and animals. And how they identified this pattern of time and life and all of existence as being a flat circle, or, as he identifies it in the following passage, a Great Wheel.

This idea didn't usually lead to a belief in reincarnation, but to the belief that what has happened before will continue to happen over and over. The moon is new, waxes, is full, wanes, and is gone. Seasons go from spring to summer to autumn to winter. People go from birth to life to death. Over and over.

He sums up the prevailing worldview like this:

> Avram[i] would have been given the same advice that wise men as diverse as Heraclitus, Lao-Tsu, and

---

[i] Cahill prefers this spelling, versus "Abram" to stay true to the original Hebrew pronunciation.

Siddhartha[ii] would one day give their followers: do not journey but sit; compose yourself by the river of life, meditate on its ceaseless and meaningless flow—on all that is past or passing or to come—until you have absorbed the pattern and have come to peace with the Great Wheel and with your own death and the death of all things in the corruptible sphere.[4]

If that's all there is to life, then nihilism makes a whole lot of sense. But Cahill points out that, in a world where this was the dominant worldview, God called Abram to something unprecedented—something *in the future.*

When we try to wrap our minds around the idea that time is a flat circle and everything keeps repeating, it's almost impossible for us to grasp the concept. The American Dream is built on the exact opposite premise, that things are not permanent but imminently changeable. When we try to think of time just being the same story over and over and over, that seems a little odd on its face. But when we apply it to our own lives, we see that we may be more like the people of the circle than we thought. Think of how often we base our current actions

---

ii These were three ancient philosophers: Heraclitus in Greece, Lao-Tsu in China, and Siddhartha (more commonly known as the Buddha) in India.

and decisions and words on what happened before. Think of the constant refrain of people who have been hurt or let down: "Yeah, I tried that already."

I'm not talking only about when it comes to the huge issue we're dealing with—pain. We use this reasoning to avoid hard conversations with our spouses or our coworkers. We use it as an excuse to not be vulnerable and honest with those around us. We use it as an excuse to stop trusting God and believing the future could be different from the present. When we look at how we live, we see we tend to get trapped in the circle.

"I tried that before and nothing changed."

If I'm honest about how I make decisions, I have to admit that sometimes I look a lot like the people of the circle. None of us would ever say we think of time as a flat circle, but we sure live like we think of it that way. And I think I'm a circle person when it comes to dealing with my health issue. I've had the same experience over and over and over. The doctors are optimistic and say they'll have me feeling better. Then, after a bunch of tests (and bills), they say they can't find anything wrong with me.

All those previous experiences are imprinted on my memory when I head into a new appointment. I was surprised when I even felt that way partway through my visit to the Mayo Clinic. I was at the top hospital system in the United States, and maybe the world, and after day one, I was stuck back in the circle. That night I told my wife, Annaliese, that I was trying to remind myself that, even though these were the same tests I'd gone through before, it was more about the fact that some of the top medical professionals in the world were reading the test results than it was about the tests themselves. But to be honest, I couldn't break myself out of circle thinking. And when they told me I was healthy and test results showed no cause for how I was feeling, I wasn't surprised. That's how these appointments had always gone.

As I've shared my own experience with others, I've found that nihilism and circle thinking are especially threatening to those of us who have had similar experiences in seeking a diagnosis, treatment, or solution. We have more reason to expect the future to look like the past than to expect otherwise. The more I've looked at my life, the more I've realized that I spend an awful lot of my time in the realm of the circle.

How Do We Break Out of Circle Thinking?

I've always appreciated the starting point of twelve-step programs. Step 1 is admitting you're powerless, that you have a problem. It's so straightforward. And it's the perfect first step because it's not all that intimidating. It's just about being honest. The real work is everything that comes after that admission. Once I admitted I had a problem with circle thinking, I started trying to be on the lookout for it in my life.

In the first week, I had several "opportunities" (they don't feel like opportunities in the moment!) to practice imagining that the future could be different from the past and the present. I had some uncomfortable conversations and confrontations with the people around me. I was quicker to confront, because I wanted to identify issues and work together to move on from them. But I was also quicker to be vulnerable in those conversations, because I wanted to keep myself open to the possibility that my health didn't have to stay the same. Week one was probably about fifty-fifty in terms of success and failure. Certainly in some moments and even days I wished I could just stay in circle land. But as I got more used to expecting and believing change was possible, I found my perspective slowly beginning to shift.

This change didn't just affect the way I interacted with people, but also the way I thought of my health. I don't want to sound like I became some naïve optimist when it came to the future, but I started to be open to how God could use what I was dealing with to make an impact on others. I finally started to think of outcomes other than a diagnosis and a solution as possibly having value.

Without that mental shift, I'm convinced that you will get stuck in the earlier stages of grief—denial, anger, bargaining, and depression—and will be unable to move to acceptance. I want to break down that process in the coming pages, because I think it's a relatable journey, and making it will help us to be less self-centered as we move forward.

Looking outside our own experience and seeing that everybody around us is dealing with pain to some degree allows us to have more grace with people. I love an anonymous quote I've seen numerous times online: "Be kind, for everyone you meet is fighting a hard battle you know nothing about." It's hard to remember that (or even care about it) when we are in deep and potentially unending pain ourselves. But remember the dignity Jesus gave his tormentors from the cross. "Father, forgive them, for they do not know what they are doing."[5] In unimaginable agony, battered beyond recognition, Jesus extended grace to the people torturing him. Obviously, a huge reason for that was to teach us how to forgive and how to show grace in every circumstance. If he hadn't done something like that, it would take the teeth out of his command to forgive an almost unlimited number of times and to love our enemies—which would've been nice, because it would have let us off the hook a bit.

Instead he doubled down on his teaching. After offering forgiveness when he had every reason not to, he went a step further and empathized with his torturers by acknowledging that their own humanity and brokenness was what had led them to do what they did. Living *that* kind of grace-filled life is what following Jesus is all about! It's an unbelievable precedent, and I'm going to take an idea from Andy Stanley here. He often says something along these lines: "I'm not asking you to do this. *I* would never ask you to do this, because it's way too hard. But that's what God is asking of us." I always appreciate that perspective, because it beautifully explains how we are all on the same level when it comes to finding Jesus's teaching to be so incredibly difficult to live out. What Jesus taught us about pain goes against every fiber of our being and everything that feels completely justified in the moment. He taught a way of seeing the world that is above and beyond anything we ever wanted to be true.

I think this is a big part of why the Way of Jesus endures century after century—he called us to do what is hard, even what seems impossible. But he also followed through with and lived out what was hard when he was on earth, so we realize he wasn't just throwing out some unlivable ideal and leaving us on our own. He backed up what he talked about with the way he lived, so we could see what it would look like for us to live with grace, forgiveness, and empathy for the brokenness of the people around us. It's the standard he set. It's the example he left. It's a high and difficult calling, but it's what he called us to.

If we allow ourselves to see the world around us in this way, we become gentler, more patient, more forgiving, more understanding, and more generous. There's no downside to any of those behaviors. But living like that requires us to let God change our hearts and our perspectives. Pain will teach us the opposite if we aren't attentive. It's easier to lash out than to give somebody the benefit of the doubt. It's easier to hold on to anger internally than to let it go and realize it doesn't benefit us in any way.

CHAPTER 2

Denial

I think the first thing Christians do when we're faced with hardship is wonder why God allowed it into our lives. As much as he can teach us in our pain, this time can also produce deep doubt, maybe even leading to a complete abandonment of God. I want to share my journey asking the *how* and *why* questions as we dig into what the denial stage looked like for me.

My experience with denial was less about denying what I was experiencing than about denying that it might be hard to identify and fix the problem, let alone be long-term. Our society doesn't value surrender or giving up. And because of that, we can extend our time of living in denial with the misguided idea that we're not quite ready to "admit defeat."

During this stage, I was optimistic in the face of feeling physically awful all the time. However, my optimism was rooted in thinking I was dealing with a temporary and changeable situation, and even though I found it to be more than a little annoying, that was nearly the end of it. I wasn't worried that these symptoms might be indicating something more serious was wrong with me, and I never even considered that I might not find a solution quickly, much less that I might not find a solution at all!

To be perfectly honest, I have to admit that denial was my favorite of the first four stages of grief. And I think that's probably the beauty of it for hurting or grieving people. Denial allows us to continue as if nothing is wrong, or at least as though nothing is *too* wrong. The comfort we take in that "reality" is what we need so desperately, and even if it's not based in reality, denial still makes us feel comforted in the moment. I'm not a psychologist, and I'm not claiming to have the ultimate advice for those who find themselves in these stages of grief, but I think people who are more honest and realistic about their situation probably move from denial to acceptance faster than those who aren't. It took me about five and a half years, so you can guess how realistic I've been.

To make my situation more complicated, I also had a hard time calling it "pain" or "suffering" because I knew there were people all over the world in much worse situations than I was.

For the most part, I guess, my form of denial was Googling the same symptoms over and over and hoping for a different result. I was searching high and low for whatever exceedingly rare syndrome or infection might be causing me to feel this way. This effort never resulted in an answer, but that didn't stop me for a while. I'm a problem-solving kind of person, so I locked into finding a diagnosis or pursuing whatever treatment option I found.

I've tried a handful of extreme diets in pursuit of discovering what might be my issue, and I was so stringent that I wouldn't even let my wife kiss me for a while after she ate for fear of potential contamination. She hated that! When I'm going after something, I'm committed to it. And this was how I approached finding a diagnosis in the beginning. I would go all in on whatever a doctor suggested, or on what some random person on the internet suggested, mostly because I refused to believe this might be a long-term health issue I would have to learn to deal with.

When people told me I needed to just go to the Mayo Clinic, I had two reasons for putting that off. The first was financial, but the second was fear of the potential for finality. In the back of my mind, I knew I couldn't keep living in denial if they said they couldn't figure out what was wrong with me. I would be doomed to live like this forever. For some reason the thought of having hope for a resolution taken off the table was even harder for me than the thought of continuing to live with it day to day.

Junietta Baker McCall describes denial this way: "The purpose of these thoughts is to protect the newly grieving person from the impact of the loss. In a sense, the person takes momentary flight from the loss."[6] This is why denial is weirdly comforting. It provides a bit of a protective shield between us and reality. By pretending our pain is not the truth, we're able to cope and to make it through daily life, adjusting to our own version of reality. When we shield ourselves from the truth like this, denial is a huge asset in helping us function…for a bit.

I'm guessing we all know or know of people who chose to live in denial for the rest of their lives after a loss, disease, or injury. From an outside perspective, it's easy to see when people have chosen to remain detached from reality because reality is too painful. When it's our own life, though, it's harder to identify because we're so close to the situation. As we're reminded so often when it comes to other people, it's easy (and natural) to edit our own histories and slant them in a way that reflects on us positively.

I love a book with an awesome title, *Mistakes Were Made (but not by* me*).* The authors focus on how we justify our behavior and edit our memories constantly so that we can fit our memories of ourselves and our actions into a cohesive story about who we are. Carol Tavris and Elliot Aronson write, "History is written by the victors, and when we write our own histories, we do so just as the conquerors of nations do: to justify our actions and make us look and feel good about ourselves and what we did or what we failed to do."[7]

Even as doctor after doctor told me I would probably have to just get used to living with this condition, I stayed in denial. I told myself they were bad at their jobs, they didn't know what they were doing, or they just weren't listening to me or taking everything into account. I told myself whatever I needed to so I could keep living in this false reality I was carefully constructing. The problem with false realities is that they must eventually come to an end, and our natural response to that is anger. But before we get to that, let's look at some biblical accounts of denial.

Jonah and Denial

I know I said in the Introduction that we would look at biblical characters thought of as positive leaders and examples as much as possible, but the story of Jonah is too good to pass up as an example of denial. The general outline of the story—commonly called "Jonah and the whale"—is familiar to anybody who ever went to Sunday school as a kid. The story turns Israel's typical confidence of being God's chosen people on its head. It's a picture of how the Bible challenges, as John Dominic Crossan says in *The Power of Parable*, "the general biblical tradition, namely, that prophets are good and obedient while Gentiles—and especially Assyrians—are bad and disobedient."[8]

Jonah fled from God's call and headed toward Tarshish. Some scholars think the modern-day location of Tarshish is on an island off Italy called Sardinia. If that was the case, Jonah not only headed in the opposite direction of where God told him to go, but traveled twice as far to do it! Without our knowing the geography and layout of the Middle East, this story can seem like just words on a page. But I want you to get what happened here. If Jonah had been in Chicago instead of Joppa when his journey began, and God had called him to Philadelphia instead of Nineveh, he would have set off to Los Angeles instead of Tarshish.

But he obviously couldn't drive or fly, so the way we think of that journey is way off too. Because I have access to airline travel, I think of Los Angeles as being five or so hours away from the middle of the country. Stanford

University developed an interactive tool called ORBIS[9] that lets you see ancient travel routes and calculate travel time in the ancient world. For Jonah to travel by boat from Joppa to Tarshish (if it was on the island of Sardinia) would have taken *nineteen days*! He was committed to this disobedience. He didn't just want to go in the opposite direction; he wanted to go *far* in the opposite direction.

To be honest, if I had been in Jonah's shoes, I'm not sure I would have behaved much differently. Nineveh was the capital of the Assyrian empire, a brutal nation-state that subjugated their enemies. They defeated surrounding nations to expand their own empire. And if they defeated you (which they did whenever they tried), they took people from your nation and moved them into surrounding nations. They also brought in people from the surrounding defeated nations and put them in your nation. This was one of their ways to ensure their defeated territories didn't try to rebel. Then they required taxes and tributes from their defeated nations, and their approach to suppressing uprisings or rebellions was unbelievably brutal. They were known for torturing rebels by flaying skin off or disemboweling living people. They sometimes killed a person's entire family in front of them and then gouged out that person's eyes to ensure that scene was the last image they ever saw. They were unbelievably vicious.

The third chapter of Nahum is a proclamation of God's coming judgment against Nineveh, and this is how that chapter ends:

> Nothing can heal you;
>   your wound is fatal.
> All who hear the news about you
>   clap their hands at your fall,
> for who has not felt
>   your endless cruelty?[10]

This was how Jonah and most of the other people alive at that time in history felt about Assyria. God saying he was going to destroy Assyria would have been great news to Jonah! We tend to think of history as being completely different from our modern lives, but we can certainly imagine the fear and anxiety that would grip us if a force like ISIS was a world-conquering power. Especially if they turned their sights to our nation occasionally. That's where Jonah was called to go. And in an act of complete (and I think honest) disobedience, he took off in the opposite direction. Intentionally.

The famous part of the story happened next. A storm on the way there threatened to wreck the ship Jonah was on. He eventually admitted it was his fault for disobeying and running from God, and he convinced the sailors to throw him overboard to save themselves. His plan worked, and the men were saved. But, unexpectedly, so was Jonah. God provided a whale or "great fish" that swallowed him, and Jonah cried out to God in the belly of this fish. He confessed his disobedience (which is a funny thought, because it's not as if it was hidden *at all*), and God had the fish spit him out. We don't know how much time elapsed from the beginning of his journey to this point, but we do know that Jonah was finally ready to obey God and go to Nineveh.

When we read the text, however, we see his attitude was different from what we'd expect from somebody God had just spared. Jonah traveled through Nineveh and preached this "sermon": "Forty more days and Nineveh will be overthrown!"[11] It doesn't seem like he put much thought or effort into that one. He didn't mention God, he didn't mention why they would be overthrown, and he didn't mention anything they could do about it. And if you think his message was short in English, it's even more shocking to find that it was only five words in the original language! Honestly, it was a pathetic version of obedience.

After he had dutifully brought his message around, the word of his preaching reached the king, who organized a nationwide fast, a time of mourning and repentance. The king wasn't even expecting a certain outcome, but said, "Who knows? God may yet relent and with compassion turn from his fierce anger so that we will not perish."[12]

And sure enough, just like God gave Jonah a second chance and met him with mercy and compassion when he was willfully disobedient, God gave Nineveh and Assyria a second chance and met them with mercy and compassion. Jonah's response to this is found near the end of the book:

> He prayed to the LORD, "Isn't this what I said, LORD, when I was still at home? That is what I tried to forestall by fleeing to Tarshish. I knew that you are a gracious and compassionate God, slow to anger and abounding in love, a God who relents from sending calamity. Now, LORD, take away my life, for it is better for me to die than to live."[13]

Jonah was absolutely choosing denial in the face of his pain. He refused to believe God would or should offer the grace he had so freely offered to Jonah to the Assyrians, the enemies of Israel and Judah. Sometimes our denial is based on that type of thinking. Instead of living and struggling with the reality of life (like Jacob wrestled with God in the night), sometimes it's easier to flat-out deny reality—to pretend like we're not really facing what we're facing, or to downplay what we're facing. I believe this is one of the spots where so many people get stuck. We just can't believe God would do certain things or allow those things to happen. But we have to allow God to do his own thing instead of trying to move him in a certain direction or control him. That's the only way to make sense of an all-powerful, all-loving God in the context of the world we experience.

Jesus and Denial

It's weird to think of handling denial in a healthy way, but here's how I think Jesus did it. His version of denial was more about staying hopeful and healthy than anything else. He didn't allow what he experienced day after day to change his mind about his mission and about the hope that God wanted people to experience. Even though he continually ran into people who weren't open to that message. He lived in denial of the reality that people didn't want to be transformed. In his case, this state made him more optimistic and more willing to complete his goals. As he constantly ran into unbelief, disobedience, and insults, he didn't let it stop him from doing what he needed to do.

When I started in full-time ministry, my biggest fear was that people wouldn't change. Rationally, I knew—and still know—that change in a positive direction isn't ultimately up to me. It's a work only God can do, and that he can do it only with a willing and obedient participant. I began in ministry knowing this truth, and trying to act according to it. I spoke publicly and talked with people about changing their lives for the better. I offered advice and challenged people. But the longer I did this, I began feeling like I was investing so much into relationships, discipleship, and accountability, yet seeing little positive outcome. As time went on, I gave less emotional energy and support to people because I stopped believing they would work to get out of a bad spot they were in. I stopped offering advice on solutions and next steps because I stopped believing people would act on my suggestions. I stopped getting excited about pointing to biblical practices and teachings because I got burned out from sharing these truths and watching people keep doing their own thing.

If I felt that way, imagine how much deeper that sense of disappointment and discouragement must have been for Jesus! He constantly ran into unbelief, disobedience, and insults, but he didn't let it stop him from doing what he needed to do. As John writes in the first chapter of his Gospel, "Though the world was made through him, the world did not recognize him. He came to that which was his own, but his own did not receive him."[14] What a heartbreaking summary of Jesus's life on earth. But I think we can all relate on a minor level. I'm sure we've all tried to help or offered advice or support in good faith and had our motivations or actions misunderstood. When we try to do good and it's misunderstood or twisted against us, the pain is significant. It usually makes us shut down and avoid trying to help in the future.

Although that's the natural response, that's what makes the Way of Jesus so genius! Despite being unrecognized and unreceived, Jesus didn't stop reaching out. He didn't stop preaching the good news! He didn't let the pain make him shut down. He didn't choose to protect himself at the expense of other people. Jesus went the opposite way: despite the reality that people didn't want to be transformed, he refused to give up. He acknowledged the reality of the situation without letting disappointment and a pessimistic outlook stop him from giving his all.

When Jesus saw the Roman centurion's faith in his ability to heal the man's servant, Jesus "was amazed"[15] and talked about how he hadn't seen faith like that in all of Israel. Despite spending nearly all of his time ministering in Israel, he saw rejection, misunderstanding, and resistance day after day rather than faith and acceptance of his message of hope. The unbelieving religious leaders constantly tried to lead Jesus into traps with their questions. He repeatedly dealt with their heckling, but he didn't shy away from teaching and healing as he moved forward. Even those closest to Jesus didn't "get it" a lot of the time. Peter walked on water, but lost faith and started to sink. When Jesus and his disciples were on a boat in the middle of a huge storm, and they were afraid (even experienced fishermen, James and John, were terrified) he said, "You of little faith."[16] These admonishments were said to his inner circle, the twelve who followed him most closely. If even they didn't get it, he must have had questions about whether he was making a difference at all!

If we forget Jesus was fully God *and* fully human, we can miss this. It's easy to say, "Well, because he was God, he knew the overall outcome. He knew he was going to have the ultimate victory." Even if that were true, we can't take the human element away from the equation. Jesus had to feel depleted by so many people missing the point and being flat-out antagonistic to his teaching.

Handling Denial Like Jesus Did

Jesus confronted these painful moments head-on. He didn't hide what was going on inside, and he didn't let that dictate his behavior. That's the healthy way of dealing with denial. It's a tricky balance, but if we model our behavior in the denial stage on Jesus's behavior, we will continue to take action that isn't completely dictated by our emotional state. As we go through the stages of grief in the journey toward acceptance, we will see that this is Jesus's course of action every time. Instead of letting this process stop him from doing what he needed to do, he allowed himself to feel the pain and loss at each stage. But he didn't let his emotional state dictate his actions. That's the challenge for us as we move through this journey of pain.

CHAPTER 3

Anger

As I mentioned, I wasn't aware I was going through the stages of grief until I came out on the other side of them. So you're going to see a surprising lack of self-awareness as I share what was going on for me internally. My hope is that you'll be able to see your own life more clearly through learning how I so badly missed the obvious.

Anger showed up in how I felt about and reacted to going from doctor to doctor, dealing with my insurance company, and talking with people around me who meant well and offered advice, comfort, and encouragement along the way. Remember the wisdom from Timothy and Kathy Keller I quoted in the Introduction? Pain makes us inward-focused and "helps" us to justify our unhealthy behavior because we rationalize and explain our actions based on our pain.

I hated the process of jumping from doctor to doctor, of having to get referrals to see specialists that may have been able to help, and at times feeling like I was the only one interested in figuring out what was wrong with me. I hated dealing with my health insurance company. I hated wasting money on test after test and treatment after treatment with nothing to show for it. I hated jumping from one extreme elimination diet to another.

This is kind of a no-brainer, but you can function only so well doing so many things you hate on top of already dealing with the actual health issue that won't go away. And while I didn't realize I was doing it at the time, I took my anger and frustration out on the people who loved me.

I rarely responded sarcastically to any of the medical professionals. I rarely lost my temper with the people from my insurance company. Not that taking it out on them would have been better, but this is just a reminder of how we tend to hurt those we love the most. I guess I knew, subconsciously, that if I burned a bridge with my local specialists, then I would be out of luck if I ever needed their help. So I showed up at their offices and *thanked them* for trying, even as my heart was breaking with the news of another wasted effort and more wasted money. Rationally, I knew it wasn't their fault, but I was hurting so much I didn't care about what I rationally knew. I was so wounded, angry, and hopeless that I went to doctors in waves. I would go through the process of seeing a couple of specialists and then be so angry and disappointed that I would need several months to regain the emotional equilibrium to be able to start the process over.

And all along I took out my anger and disappointment on the people around me.

Despite being open about my health challenge initially, after the first six months or so I got tired of talking about it because it was the same story over and over.

Yes, I feel bad *all the time*.

No, there's never any relief.

Yes, sometimes it's worse.

Yes, I've tried getting more sleep.

Yes, I've tried eating gluten-free/sugar-free/dairy-free/vegan…

Yes, I'm active and get exercise.

Yes, I've been tested for Lyme disease.

Yes, I've seen a sleep specialist.

I never had an update, so these conversations were awful for me. I felt as if I was going through the motions for everybody else's benefit when *I* was the one who should have been comforted! I felt I was tagged in people's minds for small talk. Just like you probably have a college football fan in your office or know someone really into their pets or who likes the same type of movies you do, so your go-to topic for small talk is set.

I was "the sick guy." If people couldn't think of anything else to talk about, they asked how I was feeling. I know they meant well. I know they wanted to communicate that they cared. I know they were able to be more optimistic than I was because they weren't having their optimism beaten out of them by the daily grind of life while feeling like garbage, and by doctor appointment after doctor appointment turning up nothing. I know they wanted to communicate that I wasn't alone. But to me, it was like they were saying, "Hey, let's talk about the worst part of your life for a bit."

And whenever I felt overwhelmed by having these same conversations multiple times every day, I started focusing my anger on the people around me who were "forcing" me to talk about it so often. I started shutting people out. If anybody asked me how I was feeling or if I had any updates, I would get quiet, look away, and tell them I didn't want to talk about it. I'm not a very expressive person, and I've never asked my friends and family if they knew

I was mad or hurt or frustrated in those moments, but I communicated that the topic of my health was off-limits. And I hurt some people in the process of shutting them out, but I didn't care. I was too focused on thinking about how selfish it would be for them to feel hurt when *I* was the one who *should* feel hurt!

I hope that thought process strikes you as unbelievably selfish and ridiculous. It strikes me that way—now. But it felt perfectly reasonable at the time. I felt completely justified in doing whatever I could to make other people stop talking to me about what I was going through. I wasn't in a place to have those conversations, but I didn't even have the perspective in those moments to explain that to people. I was just hurt and focusing inward, and I did some serious damage to the people who cared about me.

In his immensely helpful book *Nonviolent Communication*, Dr. Marshall Rosenberg writes, "Anger can be valuable if we use it as an alarm clock to wake us up—to realize we have a need that isn't being met and that we are thinking in a way that makes it unlikely to be met."[17] That insight would have gone a long way toward helping me do some introspection about why I was treating people so poorly in my efforts to get my needs met. Hopefully, if you're in this stage of your pain, you can use my experience and realization to be more reflective and do less damage to the people who care about you.

I wish this were the extent of how my anger hurt the people around me, but it isn't. I met my wife in May of 2013. I had been dealing with this health stuff for around two years, and I had grown *very* sick of talking to people about it. But as you can imagine, after meeting and starting to date somebody I was really interested in, I was an open book! I talked to her about how I was feeling and what potential solutions I had pursued. I brainstormed new specialists and options with her. I was great!

But as time wore on, and without having dealt with the root of my anger, I eventually got sick of talking to her about my health too. It's true that I needed space and I wasn't in a place emotionally to handle spending a lot of time talking about it, but I rarely handled that conversation maturely. I would tell her I couldn't or wasn't willing to talk about it. And whenever she said it was so hard that we had to deal with this health thing, I would get annoyed and defensive and ask what she meant when she said *we*. *I* was the one suffering. It's embarrassing to write this and to reflect on the way I caused her pain because of my own selfishness and inability to deal with my anger in a healthy way. Especially considering that my role is as a speaker for a ministry focused on marriage and family life. But I think it's important to share the reality of what can come up in this journey of pain and suffering for any of us. It's ugly, but it's real.

Unfortunately, I believe you'll be able to relate all too well to my example if you don't figure out a way to deal with your anger in a way that doesn't ignore it or minimize its impact on your life. But before we get to how to deal with your anger, let's look at a story from the life of a Bible character that tells you how *not* to deal with your anger.

Moses and Anger

When I think of anger and Bible characters, my mind is drawn quickly to Moses. His backstory is a fascinating one. He was hidden and protected by his family as a baby until, eventually, they had to give him up for his and their own safety. Pharaoh's daughter found him and took him in to be raised among Egyptian royalty, all while his own Hebrew people were enslaved. The biblical account isn't clear on whether Moses always knew of his Hebrew roots or if he came to learn of his history as he grew older, but we do know that after he grew up, he watched an Egyptian beating one of his fellow Hebrews and killed the Egyptian to stop the beating. This started his own personal exodus from Egypt, the beginning of the central Moses story.

After Egypt, Moses lived out in the wilderness, got married, and took a job as a shepherd. It was a crazy lifestyle change from being part of the royal household in Egypt, but compared to what came next, this story hadn't even gotten interesting yet! In the famous story, God spoke to Moses from a burning bush, giving Moses a call he didn't seem to want. He eventually went to Egypt in obedience to God, and God used Moses to speak to Pharaoh and free the Hebrew people. On their way out of Egypt, God parted the Red Sea, guided them by day and night, and provided food and water that often came out of nowhere.

Exodus 17 and Numbers 20 both record an instance of God providing water for the Israelite people out of a rock. Scholars disagree on whether these were two separate events or two tellings of the same event. Either way, in both accounts, the Israelites communicated a version of this complaint: "Why did you and God bring us out here to this desert with no water? If we were just going to die, we could have stayed in Egypt." To be honest, I've always felt they get the short end of the stick when all we say from these passages is, "Oh, Israel kept on complaining. They were always questioning God."

Think about the times you've been in almost unbearably hot temperatures or you've been unable to get out of direct sunlight. After a while, you're just sick of it. You're done. Now imagine you can't get any water. My mind goes to the times I've been to an amusement park like Cedar Point in Ohio in the middle of summer. You're in stagnant air. The sun's rays are hitting you from above, and they're also bouncing off the concrete and hitting you from below. Even though vendors are charging something like four dollars for a bottle of cold water, it feels like a bargain!

Let's go back to the desert with Israel. This hasn't been a temporary case of being exposed to the elements and not knowing where the next meal or drink of water may come from. They're exposed to the elements every day, and they are *completely* dependent on Moses for leadership and on God for provision. I know their example isn't one we're supposed to aim to follow, but I can see myself among the people voicing frustration to Moses.

Moses and Aaron sought a solution from God, and God told Moses to take his staff and speak to a rock, which would then start gushing water. But Moses ended up going a bit off script. Numbers 20 records what happened: "Moses said to them, 'Listen, you rebels, must we bring you water out of this rock?' Then Moses raised his arm and struck the rock twice with his staff. Water gushed out, and the community and their livestock drank."[18]

I'm a realist, so when I read this story, I can only imagine how good it felt to be Moses in that moment. He got to yell at the people who had been challenging him, and he got to make a dramatic point about how obviously wrong they were to question him and God in the first place. The problem was he was acting out of his hurt and anger. Perhaps he was annoyed and embarrassed and just wanted to get this whole thing over with. And in his anger, he didn't do what God had told him. He hit the rock instead of speaking to it. And he added his own little emotional punch with his dramatic line, "Listen, *you rebels*, must *we* bring you water out of this *rock*?" (emphases added).

Not to tarnish his image, but you can almost see Moses getting wild-eyed as he demanded the attention of everyone around him. We've all seen people completely lose control in the moment, and I don't think it's much of a stretch to imagine that's what happened here. Moses had reached his limit. He couldn't take any more questioning, complaining, and needling. He did what most of us probably would have done in his situation. He started yelling and decided to take matters into his own hands. He forgot (maybe in a moment of rage) or ignored (probably for the same reason) God's instructions and did his own thing.

Even though that's not a typical situation to be in, it's a typical response to anger. Deep emotion has a strange way of giving us tunnel vision. It makes us believe that expressing that anger, even in an unhealthy way, would feel great. When we're hurt or intensely focused on what we're dealing with, this temptation is strong. And even more than that, it feels like we'd be in the right if we exploded. But that's usually not true.

Moses's outburst and disobedience to what God told him to do had some serious consequences. In verse 12, right after the water came out of the rock, we read, "The Lord said to Moses and Aaron, 'Because you did not trust in me enough to honor me as holy in the sight of the Israelites, you will not bring this community into the land I give them.'"[19] Irreparable damage was done in a brief moment. I'm sure if we're honest with ourselves, we can all picture the damage we've done in brief moments of losing our temper, or of responding sarcastically or hurtfully out of our anger. When anger is not dealt with in a healthy way, or when it's unchecked, we do damage and we suffer the consequences.

From my personal story and from the story of Moses, we've looked at how we deal with our anger in unhealthy ways, and we've seen the damage that can do. Hopefully, you've also held up the mirror and looked at your own thoughts and actions based in unhealthy anger. When we realize the damage we've done in those moments, it's not difficult to see there must be a better way. For that, we turn to the life of Jesus.

Jesus and Anger

Jesus's most famous moment of dealing with anger is when he flipped the tables and drove the money changers away from the temple when they'd turned a place of worship into an opportunity to make a quick, and artificially inflated, buck. But let's focus on a moment that closely mirrors the Moses situation. In the second chapter of Mark, we see Jesus had run-ins with the religious leaders and the teachers of the law in several consecutive settings. He forgave and healed a paralyzed man, for which he was accused of blasphemy because only God has the power to forgive sins. Next, he was questioned for spending time with tax collectors and sinners, even eating with them. Finally, he was questioned about why his disciples weren't fasting and why they picked and ate grain on the Sabbath, which was considered work and was against the Sabbath regulations.

That's the backdrop for Mark 3, which takes place on a Sabbath. Jesus encountered a man with a shriveled hand. Knowing he was going to be involved in controversy for what he was about to do, he started with a question to his challengers: "'Which is lawful on the Sabbath: to do good or to do evil, to save life or to kill?' But they remained silent. He looked around at them in anger and, deeply distressed at their stubborn hearts, said to the man, 'Stretch out your hand.' He stretched it out, and his hand was completely restored."[20]

In a situation where he had every right to be indignant about the questioning and repeated obstacles people and life were putting in his way, Jesus did the right thing without letting his anger call the shots. He didn't try to pretend he wasn't angry. He allowed his anger to be obvious enough that Mark, who was likely getting his information from Simon Peter as an eyewitness, noticed it enough to add that he looked around *in anger*.

Jesus was experiencing anger directly related to his grief, frustration, and pain at being misunderstood so deeply. He had every right to lose control of his emotions in that moment (and I think I would have if I had been in his situation), but he expressed his anger in a healthy way. He didn't try to hide it, but he didn't let it run rampant either. Everybody around him realized he was angry, but he didn't allow that to be the main takeaway as Moses did, and as I often did—and sometimes still do.

When it feels as though everything is working against you, which is where I believe Moses and Jesus found themselves in these moments, and you're dealing with pain or suffering or loss, anger is a completely normal emotion. It's not the *feeling* of anger we should judge as healthy or unhealthy, but how we deal with that anger. Sometimes we lash out like Moses did and try to make a point or look to make examples out of the people around us. But hopefully, as we continue this journey of trying to look more and more like Jesus, we find ourselves responding that way less and less frequently.

Handling Anger Like Jesus Did

Acknowledge it.

It's okay to be angry. If you're from the Midwest like me, you might have the misconception that being nice means never admitting to yourself or to others that you're angry or frustrated, or that you feel like your input doesn't matter in the decision-making process. After being pestered and harassed at what must have felt like every turn, Jesus had reached his limit for being questioned. It's clear that he was sick of it and wanted to put a stop to it. But he didn't hide the fact that he was angry.

He didn't shy away from his emotions or feel guilty about being angry. He didn't try to justify himself or get defensive. He allowed himself to feel the anger from the comments, questioning, and misunderstanding he was facing. I believe this is a key step in the process many of us miss! If we don't allow ourselves to feel our anger and identify the root cause of that emotion, we're much more likely to take it out on people completely unconnected to our anger. If we don't deal with it in a healthy way, anger *will* spill out into other areas of our lives, and we will take it out on innocent bystanders (most likely our family members and close friends) who will be completely blindsided.

Allow yourself to express it.

This might feel like a stretch for you, but it's clear that the people around Jesus knew he was angry. Again, the prevailing understanding is that Mark wrote his Gospel using Peter as his eyewitness. When Peter told Mark this story, he remembered Jesus was angry in that moment and hadn't tried to pretend he wasn't. The key is that he expressed his anger, and he did it in a healthy way. He didn't rail against the people who had been constantly questioning him. He didn't try to "punish" them with his words or tell them to stop talking. But he did let them know he was angry. If we admit to ourselves that we're feeling anger and we allow ourselves to sit in that emotion, our actions will come from a much different place than if we don't recognize our anger or try to deny that emotion. If we don't let ourselves feel it, we are still angry, but we're not giving ourselves the opportunity to deal with it in a healthy way. Jesus was angry, but he was still in control of his actions and thoughts. That's our model for expressing our own anger.

Do what you can.

As we'll see throughout these examples from Jesus's life, he didn't let the emotions he was dealing with stop him from doing what he had set out to accomplish. Instead of being distracted from the healing he was offering to this guy who needed it so badly, he dealt with his anger head-on and then stayed on track for his goals. Too often we allow anger to sidetrack us. This can lead to missing out on experiencing life. I can't even count all the times I've been distracted by feeling like I needed to make my point or prove my point. When we're acting out of anger in an unhealthy way, we can easily get so caught up in letting everybody else know we're right, that we become distracted by disagreements and arguments that serve only to draw us further away from taking healthy action.

CHAPTER 4

The *Why* of Suffering and Pain

One of the most significant questions we ask as we deal with pain and suffering is, "Why?" I placed this chapter in the middle of the book because we will find ourselves questioning all throughout our pain journey, and we will not find a satisfactory answer. People with deeper experience and way more insight and wisdom than I possess have wrestled with this question for as long as humanity has been around. Pain doesn't make sense, especially when we try to square the existence of a good, loving God with the reality of pain and suffering we see all over the world.

C. S. Lewis is one of those people whose depth and breadth of insight and wisdom continually baffle me. In *The Problem of Pain*, he writes that the existence of free will inevitably leads to pain. He says if God were to intervene to stop evil at every opportunity, that would create a world where we would be unable to function.

> We can, perhaps, conceive of a world in which God corrected the results of this abuse of free will by His creatures at every moment: so that a wooden beam

> became soft as grass when it was used as a weapon, and the air refused to obey me if I attempted to set up in it the soundwaves that carry lies or insults. But such a world would be one in which wrong actions were impossible, and in which, therefore, freedom of the will would be void; nay, if the principle were carried to its logical conclusion, evil thoughts would be impossible, for the cerebral matter which we use in thinking would refuse its task when we attempted to frame them.[21]

He doesn't try to explain away the disconnect we sometimes face when we think of an all-powerful God who allows so much suffering. If God lets us choose our actions—even actions that damage ourselves or others—then pain is not only a possibility but a certainty. This is because we all choose the selfish option from time to time, even if we know it hurts others.

That's one way of looking at the *why* of pain and suffering. Another perspective comes from *When Suffering Persists* by Frederick W. Schmidt Jr.

> For those who suffer and believe in God, one of the most difficult challenges we can face arises out of questions about the role of God. If God is good, why doesn't God come to my aid? And if God is

powerful, why doesn't God exercise that considerable power on my behalf? Is God just not there? Or did I do something to displease God? The difficulty in answering questions of this kind can plunge us into depression, precipitate a "crisis of faith," lead us to deny the reality of our suffering, or burden us with anxiety and guilt. But what if God isn't, first and foremost, about power—or even goodness as we understand it? What if God's passion is the establishment of relationship?[22]

I assume we've all found comfort in both these ideas from deep thinkers who have methodically explained the existence of pain. But this chapter is less about giving an answer to the why question than about describing what it feels like to ask why. This keeps the discussions of our emotional state and desire for healing in the context of real life. As much as we want to spend time wondering why this is happening or if there even is a God, we can relate to Tim VanDuivendyk, who wrote a book titled *The Unwanted Gift of Grief* after his infant son died. He says, "We often wonder why God is silent. In the wilderness, we often have faith struggles as we vacillate between faith and doubt, hope and despair, and courage and fear."[23]

Strangely enough, I had a big crisis of faith before I started to deal with my personal version of the question, "Why?"

Thinking about pain on a personal level is what makes it hit home for each of us individually. But any discussion of pain is entirely incomplete without addressing the pain throughout our world that results from extreme poverty, genocide, disease, war, hate, and many other causes. As we've already seen, the thing about dealing with pain on a personal level is that it makes us inward focused, which is an entirely rational and natural response. When I'm hurting, the first thing I do is go into protection mode. I need to identify what's causing my pain, and I need to focus all my energy on stopping that pain. It's a normal response, and it's a healthy response for the most part. The problem is that it can cause us to miss the learning opportunity pain presents, and it can make us miss the opportunity to minister to the people in pain around us.

Almost immediately, looking at the worldwide scale of pain becomes nearly impossible. If you go to well-respected sources to find information about the number of people who die daily from AIDS, malaria, malnutrition, drinking non-potable water, and other preventable and treatable causes, it's heartbreaking. My first experience with great pain, resulting in that crisis of faith, was on a trip to South Africa to minister to people affected by the HIV/AIDS pandemic in sub-Saharan Africa. You can look up the statistics and see what's going on in that region still today, but statistics rarely touch our hearts.

Those numbers stopped being simply statistics for me when I spent some time doing ministry in townships around Johannesburg and saw a stark contrast between how the people of color lived and how the white people lived. (The people of color originated from the Zulu, Xhosa, Southo, and several other tribes, as well as Indian people who had immigrated across the Indian Ocean; white people are there because South Africa was colonized by the Dutch in 1652.) I learned about the history of apartheid and saw firsthand that even though the official, government-sanctioned segregation came to an end in the early 1990s, the aftereffects were still causing devastation.

To boil it down to an easy-to-understand explanation, roughly 80 percent of the people in South Africa (any people of color) were forced to live on roughly 13 percent of the land. Non-white people were forced to carry ID cards or wear a badge stating their race, and these ID cards and badges were used to oppress them and dictate where they could go and when. And again, although apartheid officially ended in the early 1990s, the unequal distribution of wealth, property, and access to opportunities is still devastating lives today.

Before I even got to South Africa, I knew generally what apartheid was all about, but as I spent more time in the country, I saw its impact everywhere. I saw people living in shacks (made of whatever materials they could piece together) with no electricity or access to clean water. You don't have to work hard to imagine how horrific conditions quickly get when your only water source is contaminated with garbage, animal and human waste, and runoff from the surrounding, overpopulated areas.

That was the environment we ministered in. I encountered pain and suffering on a level I had never imagined. I saw people physically wasting away from disease, orphaned kids all over the place from a mix of AIDS and extreme poverty, and all the other problems compounded by those issues. In my first week there, our group was praying with a woman in the final stages of tuberculosis, laying hands on her, when she died. I wasn't expecting anything like that, and I definitely wasn't mentally or emotionally prepared for it. Ten years since that moment, I've had conversations with a few of the other people there that day, and we all remember it vividly. In separate conversations, multiple people have described how "something broke" inside of them, and I would echo that.

The Why of Suffering and Pain

I spent a year doing ministry in South Africa among beautiful people living in terrible conditions, and I never could quite make sense of the pain and suffering. It didn't fit into any view of God I was comfortable with. Once back in the United States, I heard people talk about how God helped them get a good parking spot or how he helped some team win a basketball game, and I was offended. If there was a God who cared about that stuff, but he also allowed people to die from preventable and treatable diseases, I didn't want to follow that God. And I was really open about that whenever people talked about God helping them make a putt or get a raise.

My view of the way God interacted with the world became minimal. I started thinking that just as he set up natural forces that cause hurricanes and earthquakes and tornadoes, he allowed people's influence on our world to cause harm and natural consequences. War and apartheid and discrimination and violence fit into my worldview of a God who started the world in motion and then rarely stepped in to make changes—even to change bad things.

I think living there for a year, face-to-face with the reality of suffering on a scale I will never be able to wrap my head around, gave me a bit of a jump-start on wrestling with the crisis of faith pain confronts us with. My own health journey didn't bring me to this point, because I'd already been brought to that point of questioning by seeing the pain and suffering of others.

This may seem strange, but I came to a resolution by reading Joseph Campbell's *The Hero with a Thousand Faces*, where he writes about creation myths from different religions as well as fables and fairy tales that have surprising commonalities across all cultures and belief systems. He wrote about God's interaction with Job, and he says this about the end of Job's story:

> There is no word of explanation, no mention of the dubious wager with Satan described in chapter one of the Book of Job; only a thunder-and-lightning demonstration of the fact of facts, namely that man cannot measure the will of God, which derives from a center beyond the range of human categories. Categories, indeed, are totally shattered by the Almighty of the Book of Job, and remain shattered to the last. Nevertheless, to Job himself the revelation appears to have made soul-satisfying sense. He was a hero who, by his courage in the fiery furnace, his unreadiness to break down and grovel before a popular conception of the character of the All Highest, had proven himself capable of facing a greater revelation than the one that satisfied his friends. We cannot interpret his words

of the last chapter as those of a man merely intimidated. They are the words of one who has *seen* something surpassing anything that has been *said* by way of justification…For the son who has grown really to know the father, the agonies of the ordeal are readily borne; the world is no longer a vale of tears but a bliss-yielding, perpetual manifestation of the Presence.[24]

It didn't fit into my previous way of thinking, but this passage challenged me to understand that faith is what is sometimes called transrational. Instead of thinking faith and rationality are two different ways of viewing the world that need to co-exist, which had been the way I was viewing the world, transrationality allows for what was never meant to be gauged as rational or irrational to just be. In this passage, Campbell is saying that God doesn't explain himself because what he does is often above and beyond what we could fit into a rational explanation. That doesn't make it irrational; it just means we can't line up everything and account for every decision and situation.

After seeing pain and suffering played out on a large scale, and also understanding that people live in abject poverty without access to adequate food and water, medical care, shelter, and other vital resources in *tons* of other places in the world, I had decided that God must not be actively involved. That was the only rational explanation for me. However, when I realized I didn't need to rationalize and figure out exactly when and how God was or wasn't at work, a huge weight was lifted from my shoulders. A weight I was never meant to carry in the first place.

Coming face-to-face with true suffering, like that in South Africa, changed me. It didn't exactly become the bar I used to measure all experiences, but it did serve as a framework for the way I understood my experiences. It changed my perspective, because I had learned there were people who took seriously Paul's words in the book of Philippians: "I have learned the secret of being content in any and every situation, whether well fed or hungry, whether living in plenty or in want."[25] I had seen it in person. People living in dire circumstances had such hope and life and joy. Obviously, they weren't finding their value or their hope or their comfort in what was going on around them, but in something else.

I've heard this experience echoed over and over from Americans who have participated in short-term or long-term ministry in developing nations. Even though we may say we find our comfort or our strength in God, when we're faced with people who have *only* God to rely on, we realize how much comfort and value we tend to find in our circumstances.

Moses knew this when he was leading the people of Israel. In Deuteronomy 8, we see him give a farewell address because he knows his time of leading the nation is limited. As we saw in the chapter on anger, he had disobeyed God during their time wandering in the wilderness, so God told him he wouldn't get to enter the promised land as punishment. Knowing this might be one of his last times to address the nation, Moses gave the Israelites a history lesson and reminded them of how God had protected them while they were in the wilderness. They had been wandering for forty years, so he was talking to two whole generations of people who didn't even remember God leading them out of Egypt or parting the Red Sea for them to cross. They remembered how God had been sustaining them in the wilderness, but they had known only one way of living—desert living. They didn't have a permanent place to live, and they were sustained only by what God provided on a day-by-day basis. Now look at how Moses described their future.

> Observe the commands of the LORD your God, walking in obedience to him and revering him. For the LORD your God is bringing you into a good land—a land with brooks, streams, and deep springs

> gushing out into the valleys and hills; a land with wheat and barley, vines and fig trees, pomegranates, olive oil and honey; a land where bread will not be scarce and you will lack nothing; a land where the rocks are iron and you can dig copper out of the hills.[26]

Most of us reading these words live in a place that makes this description of the promised land sound like a significant downgrade from our current situation. But imagine how incredible that place would sound if all you'd known for the past forty years was roving from place to place and eating manna with a bit of quail mixed in for a brief period. You don't have to wonder where to find drinkable water. You don't have to eat the same thing day after day after day. You don't need to set up portable shelters and then keep moving them around. You can get established and figure out how to settle down. Finally!

But knowing what might come about as a result of these new conditions, Moses goes on.

> When you have eaten and are satisfied, praise the LORD your God for the good land he has given you. Be careful that you do not forget the LORD your God, failing to observe his commands, his laws and his decrees that I am giving you this

day. Otherwise, when you eat and are satisfied, when you build fine houses and settle down, and when your herds and flocks grow large and your silver and gold increase and all you have is multiplied, then your heart will become proud and you will forget the LORD your God, who brought you out of Egypt, out of the land of slavery.[27]

This is not a statement in praise of pain and discomfort, but Moses understands that when everything is going great, it's much easier to lose sight of how God is constantly providing for and sustaining us.

That's one of my biggest takeaways from my time in South Africa. When life is tough, it's much easier and more natural for us to rely on God. When we realize we don't have many other options, we're happy to call out to him for help. But when a hardship takes a turn for the better, it's easy to think we're smarter than everybody else or that we were in the right place at the right time, rather than being mindful of our continual need for sustenance from God's hand.

As I said before, and as I'll keep saying throughout this book, I wish this wasn't the case. I wish we didn't learn more from pain than we do from periods of comfort and peace and ease. But experience shows over and over that we do. Whether you're stuck in one stage of grief because you don't want to come to grips with the reality of your loss, diagnosis, non-diagnosis, relationship status, or some other form of pain and suffering outside your control; or because you don't rate your current situation as qualifying as "real pain" because you know other people have it worse than you do; or for some other reason that feels completely justified and rational to you…regardless of what has stopped you up to this point, it's important to admit what you're dealing with. Being angry about your situation or denying what you're facing will not make it go away, and it won't make it hurt less. But it *will* keep you from growing, and it will keep you far away from experiencing the relief and peace that comes with acceptance.

CHAPTER 5

Bargaining

My health issue hits me in an especially devastating way because I live so much of my life thinking, reading, and writing. Because of that, I always felt like I had a little extra ammunition when it came to bargaining. Because I don't believe guilt and manipulation work as motivators, I didn't see what I was doing as bargaining at the time. I never said straight up to God, "If I'm going to keep speaking and serving you like this, you need to fix me." But I did say, "God, you know how this issue is limiting my ability to prepare sermons, to think creatively, and to read and research. I could do such a better job if I was healthy."

Reading that now, I can see there's not much difference between those two "requests," but I always convinced myself I was avoiding treating God like a genie or trying to manipulate him into the action I was hoping he'd take. Whether we make a straight-up offer to God or we just try to remind him of a few things we'd like to make sure he factors into his decision-making process, we're bargaining. The appeal of bargaining is that it's a way for us to feel like we're gaining some leverage or control over the situation.

This may be a strange way to get that idea across, but I've always gotten along really well with kids. At gatherings, family or otherwise, it's common to find me hanging out with them instead of the adults. I've always thought it's interesting how kids don't do much in the way of small talk or those social niceties of the adult world. Most of the time, kids don't even bother to ask me what my name is! And if they do, they forget it in seconds. They don't pretend to like you if they don't. They don't pretend to be interested in what you did over the weekend. They don't step aside and let you choose the game or toy the group will play with. They know what they want and they go after it.

As an adult hanging out with kids, you serve a few functions for them: you give permission for what they want to do because you're old enough to be the one in charge, you help them do things or get to places they couldn't on their own, or you become a prop for whatever story they want to tell or game they want to play. I always thought their honesty about those desires was why I was so drawn to children. They have no pretense; they don't go out of their way to act like you're important to them for any reason other than helping them maximize their own enjoyment.

An interaction with my three-year-old nephew made me rethink bargaining.

Jackson had a Matchbox car similar in design to a Ford Model T, and when I told him a Model T was "a really, really old car," he ran with it. Anytime I saw him, he brought out that car and showed me the really, really old car—often creating much hilarity. It's so funny to watch the way kids latch onto stuff.

One night I showed Jackson a video of a Ford Model T because by then he and I had a sort of bond over these really, really old cars (even though I know next to nothing about cars). I told him Henry Ford invented that car and then produced it.

"Why?" he asked.

"Because he wanted to get around faster."

"Why?"

"Because they used to ride horses."

"Why?"

"That was the best way to get from place to place."

"Why?"

"Horses were strong enough to carry people and fast enough to get them around."

"Why?"

"Well, have you ever seen a person riding a horse?"

"Why?"

"No, I'm asking you a real question."

"Yeah, I have."

"That's why they made cars. That was the first car ever invented."

"Why?"

"Because cars didn't exist at that point."

"Why?"

"You know the car your mom drives around?"

"Yeah."

"Well, the really, really old car is the first version of that."

"Why?"

And then we did some Google searches so I could show him some cars. The "Why?" game has never bothered me because it's just kids being kids. They're curious and they're stubborn, and I'm curious and stubborn, too, so I can sit there all night and keep giving answers. It's oddly entertaining to me.

When my wife and I got home, I laughed and told Annaliese about Jackson's "Why?" barrage. The next day I got hit with a powerful (and unwanted!) insight about myself. I was again laughing about Jackson and thought, *Man, he's really willful.* In the next moment, I had the realization—or God revealed to me—that I get along with kids so well because I see my willfulness reflected in them. In a strange way, I think I admire them for it.

When kids are forced to do something they don't want to do, they pout, whine, and fight; we haven't socialized them into hiding their greed and envy and controlling nature for fear of missing out on social connections. They might do it eventually, but they'll be clear that they don't want to do it. And a lot of times, I do the same. I guess I have always seen humility and submission as exactly that:

doing something you didn't want to do anyway rather than dealing with the selfishness in your core. Generally that's what my "submission" looks like on my best day. I've got my arms crossed and I'm pouting. I'm going to do what God's telling me to do, just not without letting him know I'm not happy about it.

And when I'm not submitting to God, I bargain with him. When we engage in bargaining, our goal is often to twist God's arm into doing what we want him to do.

One of the biggest lessons God has taught me through this health issue has been just how desperate I am to be in control. That's been a strange lesson, because I've never thought of myself as a control freak. Maybe the people around me would disagree!

As my wife and I were in the dating and engagement stages of our relationship, I think I did a good job of avoiding needing to be in control, at least on a small scale. But we both love to be in control, and the main place this shows up, oddly enough, is when we're cooking together. When we were dating, cooking was one of our favorite shared activities. We truly *loved* to go grocery shopping together to buy ingredients. We had a blast laughing our way through plenty of recipes, often substituting and eyeballing measurements along the way. However, over time and into our marriage, we realized we hovered over each other's shoulders more often as we were cooking. Our trust in each other looked like it was taking a step backward the longer we were married. We couldn't figure out what was going on, because it didn't make sense for me to "check in" on Annaliese's part of the recipe when I had my own melting and mixing and measuring to do. Nor did it make sense for her to "check in" on me.

But that's exactly what we started to do. We checked up on each other and helpfully (at least, it felt that way to the "helper") offered suggestions on the best way to make less of a mess, or to thoroughly mix ingredients, or to coat a pan with cooking oil. It was ridiculous. A hobby we used to love doing together had turned into a chore, all because we both loved to be in control!

When I saw my desire for control played out in such a small and insignificant way, I started noticing it in other aspects of my life. Some of those ways were much more significant, and the most glaring was how out of control I felt with my health situation.

I spent time reflecting on Isaiah 45:9 about the clay not asking the potter why he made it like that. I realized I was the clay, constantly asking why, not only trying to get God to consider a different way, but trying to rationalize my request. I reminded him of how I could be different if he would just give me the chance. How I could accomplish more. How much more effective I'd be if my brain functioned the way it's supposed to and if I had the energy and desire to do things. I was bargaining because I wanted to feel as though I had some small level of control.

In *The Unwanted Gift of Grief*, Tim VanDuivendyk explains bargaining this way:

> When we were children, we naturally had a self-centered or self-focused view of the world. We thought if good things happened, it was because we made them happen by being good. If bad things happened, we concluded we made them happen because we were bad. This self-focused thinking is normal behavior in childhood development. It may reappear in adult trauma, intense fear, or profound pain. In a crisis, adults frequently regress back to childhood feelings and thinking. This is usually caused by fear and anxiety when we pray for the cup to be lifted and it is not.[28]

That's what it is. As I've mentioned, I didn't even realize I was going through these stages of grief until I got through them all, which was why I wasn't finding effective resources and reading books about dealing with grief until after the fact. Now that I'm thinking back over the past five plus years with this perspective, I see how blatantly childish and selfish my reactions and responses were at various stages. It's embarrassing, but it's also freeing to label my words, thoughts, and actions in such an honest way. If you're seeing more of your own story than you'd like reflected in mine, don't run from that. Don't downplay the similarities between our unhealthy responses. Life is a journey, and we're all working on growing along the way.

Let the past be what it is. It's tempting to try to rewrite the past to make ourselves look good, but it doesn't help us. Unless we deal with the ugliness and immaturity in our lives, we'll keep repeating the same behavior. If we don't learn from the past, we'll keep making the same mistakes.

Abraham and Bargaining

Bargaining happens when we insert ourselves as a potential solution to a situation not within our control. When I think of that and scan through the list of Bible characters in my mind, Abraham jumps out as an example of somebody who tried to use bargaining as a solution to his problem. In the very beginning of Abraham's story, he was going by the name Abram and living in a well-off spot. He was born in the land of Ur, a place we don't really know much about, and then he moved with his father's family and his wife, Sarai, to the city of Haran. We know this city was most likely on a trade route, and in the ancient world it was a successful urban center with wealth and a strong religious grounding in the worship of the Sumerian gods. Genesis 12 records God's call to Abram:

> Go from your country, your people and your father's household to the land I will show you. I will make you into a great nation, and I will bless you; I will make your name great, and you will be a blessing. I will bless those who bless you, and whoever curses you I will curse; and all peoples on earth will be blessed through you.

And to Abram's great credit, the next verse tells us, "So Abram went, as the Lord had told him."[29]

The biblical account makes a point of saying he was seventy-five years old when he left Haran, which means the promise that he would be made "into a great nation" seemed unlikely. He was getting up there in years. And we were told before the call that Sarai, also now up in years, was childless. To be childless in the ancient world was a big deal. If you died without a son, your name and legacy wouldn't be passed on. Everything you had spent your life accumulating would end up meaning nothing because it wouldn't be given to your family to guarantee continued success.

It's staggeringly hard to make our minds think the way Abram and Sarai and their entire world thought. As a result of living in an individualist culture, not a collectivist culture, we generally think in terms of individual successes and failures. It's not that we don't care about whether we have children or whether we can pass anything along to them in terms of material wealth or goods, but we don't view childlessness the same way the ancients did. It was a deeply personal loss for them. If having many children was viewed as a blessing from the gods, then think of how childlessness reflected the opposite.

This is the backdrop for Abram and Sarai trying to make themselves the solution to their own problem and strike a deal, indirectly, with God. They saw the outcome they wanted, the same outcome we all see and want for ourselves. They wanted the pain to be over. Not much could be more understandable than that. But unlike us, they had a direct promise from God to fall back on. He had promised to make Abram into a great nation. Just like we do, Abram and Sarai tried to interpret God's words in the way that made the most sense to them. God had made that promise in a conversation with Abram, so they thought Abram might be the only vital component.

They could do the math: old man + old woman = no chance at a baby.

But they figured they had a solution: old man + not an old woman = some chance at a baby.

Despite what they had seen and heard from God, they jumped in and tried to take control of the situation. In the Genesis account, Abram reminded (complained to) God that he was childless and said, "You have given me no children; so a servant in my household will be my heir."[30] God's response was to reassure him: "This man will not be your heir, but a son who is your own flesh and blood will be your heir."[31] Then God showed him the stars in the sky and said his descendants would be as unable to be counted as the stars were.

However, nearly immediately after this, Sarai had the same line of thinking and came up with a plan. She told Abram, "The LORD has kept me from having children. Go, sleep with my slave; perhaps I can build a family through her."[32] Out of desperation, and with a little tweaking and twisting of God's words, they convinced themselves somebody needed to do something if this was ever going to happen! And even though they didn't involve God in the decision making in this, it's clear they still intended for him to be a part of the plan. In the moment they probably felt completely confident they were doing what they could to advance what God had promised and planned. That's the most damaging part of bargaining. It gives us all the control while we still pay lip service to letting God be in control.

After the birth of Abram and Sarai's son Isaac, Hagar and her son through Abram, Ishmael, lived a life of rejection, conflict, and disappointment—a result of Abram and Sarai trying to take control. And Abraham was the father of the Jewish people, the guy many of us immediately think of as an example of faith. In fact, the author of Hebrews 11, "The Faith Chapter," spends more verses talking about Abraham than any other biblical character. But even Abraham grabbed back control as he tried to bargain for the painless outcome of having an heir.

And Abram and Sarai's plan did work, bringing about their solution their way! Abram had Ishmael, an heir of his own flesh and blood. But there's an important lesson from this part of the story. Ishmael wasn't the promised son God was talking about, and we see how much pain arose because of Abram and Sarai's taking back control.

Jesus and Bargaining

Thinking of Jesus going through an experience that would fit into the category of bargaining seems strange. But I do think it's fair to look at his prayer experience in the garden of Gethsemane as an example of a healthy version of bargaining. He famously prayed, "My Father, if it is possible, may this cup be taken from me." But, beautifully, he didn't end there. He went on to pray, "Yet not as I will, but as you will."[33] My moments of submission generally look a lot less submissive than that! Jesus does "bargaining" in the garden in the healthiest way imaginable.

He knew what was coming up next for him, and even though he asked his Father for an alternative, he didn't try to negotiate a better deal. In that moment he displayed a level of maturity and obedience that is almost incomprehensible. He knew he was going to be betrayed, arrested, tried, tortured, and murdered. He knew that's what would happen next if he submitted, and he still did. He didn't try to hold out for a different or better deal. He didn't agree to part of the plan and then try to get away from some of its nastier parts ahead.

What he showed, even in his bargaining experience, was an ultimate submission to the will of God. We may try to add in the complexity of our situation and explain it away by saying we don't have the benefit he had of knowing what comes next if we submit. But, obviously, he didn't make his decision *based on* what would come next. He had every reason to fight against having to go through that, but he submitted and was obedient to his Father's will.

Handling Bargaining Like Jesus Did

Acknowledge it.

It's okay to want a different outcome than the one you're facing, and it's okay to admit that. Jesus didn't pretend he was okay with what was coming next for him. He easily could have put on a brave face and showed us the way to deal with pain in our lives is to grin and bear it. But, just the opposite, he made no effort to hide his feelings, and he didn't try to suck it up for our benefit. Interestingly, "in both of the historic creeds of the early church (the Apostles' and the Nicene Creeds), the only word that depicts the *life* of the Christ as distinct from his birth, death, resurrection, and kingly reign, is the word *suffered*."[34] Jesus knew the distinguishing moments of his life on earth would be from those final few days, and he wasn't pretending to look forward to them.

Allow yourself to express it.

Jesus moved from internally acknowledging that he wanted a different future outcome to verbalizing it. There's nothing wrong with saying we'd rather be in a different situation. Sometimes it feels as though people in the church use these little phrases that, taken literally, seem to give control back to God. But they don't use them as though that's what they really mean. Think about it. We pray for healing and then tack on at the end, "if it's your will." But we don't usually mean that. We just think we're supposed to say it. The difference between what we mean when we say that and what Jesus meant when he said it is significant. He said he wished his circumstances and calling could be different, but he ended by submitting to God's will. Whenever I've prayed "if it's your will," I've mainly been saying it to give God an "out" in case he doesn't answer my prayer the way I want him to.

Do what you can.

Again, we see that Jesus's willingness to acknowledge his emotional state and to express it allowed him to move forward without his pain and questions dictating his actions. He didn't allow his desire for a different outcome to paralyze him into inaction. He didn't hide to put off surrendering to God's will after he said he'd be willing to surrender. He avoided shortcuts and getting stalled in the bargaining phase by dealing with his circumstances head-on, ultimately willing to surrender control.

CHAPTER 6

Depression

This stage had the most negative impact on my life, but I think part of the reason was my reluctance to do anything about it. About four or so years into dealing with my undiagnosed health issue, I started feeling emotionally flat. I didn't find joy in what I had always found joy in. I felt aimless whenever I got home from work and didn't have a plan or schedule to keep that evening. And when I did have a plan or schedule, I dreaded whatever was on the docket. It almost didn't even matter what the plan was. Going for a walk with Annaliese: I wasn't in the mood. Hanging out with some of my best friends: it felt like too much work. Speaking: for the first time in my life, I went to some speaking engagements wanting them to just be over.

I stopped doing anything other than the most basic upkeep around the house. I planned activities so I'd have to spend the least amount of time possible around other people. I rarely felt up to going out on dates with Annaliese. I mostly stopped watching NBA basketball games. I got annoyed with people when I got cut off while driving or somebody wasn't driving as fast as I wanted them to. Every day of life felt like a chore. And if anything didn't go the way I had hoped it would, I found myself thinking, *No, not this too!*

It's hard to put into words, but I felt like I was sort of floating through life, or I was watching a movie about myself. My attitude toward life before this mystery illness was very much to go with the flow and let things happen without letting them rattle me. But depression fundamentally changed the way I viewed the world. I saw everything through a negative lens. Previously, I had a neutral starting point, but depression shifted the starting point to negative for almost everything. Instead of giving the benefit of the doubt and assuming other people meant well, my mind would immediately grab the potential negative meaning or intent behind a word or action.

Despite what was obvious to everyone around me, I was reluctant to describe what I was dealing with as depression. In my mind, because my mood issue was directly related to not having an answer to what was causing my health issues, this was different from clinical depression. I thought if I could just pinpoint a cause, I wouldn't need to spend time dealing with what I viewed as a side effect of my main problem.

Because of that stubbornness, it was a year of what felt like living my life in black and white instead of in color before I finally took steps to get help. Toward the beginning of my time of depression, a doctor told me I sounded like I was depressed. He was echoing what Annaliese and some other people close to me had already said. I told him I probably was, but I didn't want to treat that symptom because it was only a side effect of what I was dealing with rather than one of the main symptoms of my issue. With that bad decision I caused myself a lot more pain than necessary.

In fairness, it wasn't *only* stubbornness that caused me to want to ignore the depression. Part of my hesitancy to look into medications was that I didn't want weird side effects. I was wary that they might make it even harder to diagnose my symptoms, or that they might amplify them somehow. I was also hesitant because a friend who had gone on some medication experienced a dramatic personality change. When he went on a different medication, his mood improved, but it had been jarring and disorienting to be around him when his behavior was so dramatically different from what it had been. He was like a completely different person. I was afraid the same thing might happen to me. I didn't want to become a different person; I just didn't want to be so depressed. I didn't want to live life always feeling like anything that went wrong (or just went differently from what I had pictured) was one more thing I needed to deal with. I didn't have the emotional reserves for it.

When I was finally brutally honest with myself, I admitted that I had gone from a reserved, go-with-the-flow guy to an anxious, easily frustrated person I didn't like. I had to let it get to the point where my frustration outweighed my fears about the negative impact of going on antidepressants. I talked with multiple counselors (a huge benefit of being part of a ministry with more than fifteen counselors is getting free five-minute sessions when I catch them getting coffee!) and multiple other people in my life who were on antidepressants about their own experiences. After more than nine months of living with depression on top of my regular brain fog/fatigue/dizziness, I finally set up an appointment with my doctor.

Explaining my own journey with depression is in no way an attempt to give medical advice. Counseling and working with my doctor extensively got me to the point of realizing that antidepressants made sense for me, even given the potential side effects. I didn't make this decision lightly, and this is not me giving advice or a stamp of approval for any path to mental health. What I *do* recommend if you're dealing with depression is speaking with a counselor and a medical doctor.

Depression made me uninterested in much of life, but I slowly felt that cloud dissipate after I had been on antidepressants for around a week or ten days. I don't know if I see it as a long-term solution, but for now, it's a hugely helpful tool in feeling like I have some normalcy back in my life. In the next chapter, I'll explain what else I started doing that had a huge impact on my ability and willingness to move forward.

Kindred Spirits

As strange as it sounds, one of the highlights of life when you're in pain and experiencing depression is finding a fellow sufferer. Obviously, that's not because you're glad to hear other people are dealing with pain, but because it's an opportunity for you to know a kindred spirit. I've found spending time with fellow sufferers is unbelievably life-giving! In my experience, they offer fewer suggestions on how to fix your issues and more empathy and suggestions for coping techniques. Talking with these people who share my experience to some degree, I've found a wisdom and depth to their input I didn't find in other conversations about my health issues.

Their empathy, prayers, and encouragement carry so much more weight for me. I think it's because I know they can fully relate, maybe not to my specific condition, but to how these waves of emotion hit so unexpectedly and so frequently. I've had a long-term debate with my dad over the years about the ability to relate to other people and to understand where they're coming from. A line he loves to use is, "I guess you just have to be forty years old to understand." And as he got older, that advancing magic number stayed exactly as unattainable for me to reach. I always thought of it as a "get out of jail free" card he used whenever he couldn't explain his position well enough, or when I had proved him wrong. He seems to love pulling the line out to leave me on the wrong side of the discussion, and it drives me crazy!

But as I've connected with these kindred spirits, I've realized there is something to be said for shared experience. I'm sure some have given me the exact same encouragement or explanation my wife has given me, yet I find more comfort in what they have to say. I'm sure that drives her crazy too! But there's something about knowing other people are living with chronic pain or chronic fatigue or a terminal diagnosis or the loss of a loved one that reminds us we're not alone. And in those moments, I think there's a beauty to the book of Job, which deals with undeserved suffering. Again, Cahill's wisdom shines through on the question of unmerited suffering:

> But the question has no answer, only: "The LORD gives and the LORD takes away: Blessed be the Name of the LORD." They have reached that mysterious core of human life where one heart in pain speaks to another—and the other can respond in sympathy but without an answer. If there is a reason, it is a reason beyond reason.[35]

When I find myself around other hearts in pain, I don't find solutions. I don't find explanations. I don't even find hope. I find kindred spirits. It turns out, sometimes that's needed more than anything else.

Knowing how these kindred spirits have made an impact on me, I've tried to be intentional about seeking out people who are in pain and investing in them. And as I've come to the place of being open to talking with other people about what I've been dealing with, I've been shocked by how many people I could relate to as a result of my own experiences. Even though it seems obvious now that I think about it, I allowed my pain to make me inward focused instead of even considering how other people might be affected by their own struggles. But as tempting as it was for me to let my pain keep me inward focused all the time, when I started sharing my experience with depression and pain, God used those conversations to touch the people in pain around me.

Every single time I've shared about my undiagnosed health issue in a sermon or a speech, at least one person has come to me to talk about something they or one of their loved ones is dealing with. That's been so helpful in breaking me out of staying focused on just me. Even at the beginning, what I said to everybody who tried to console me about having no answer was, "Well, everybody deals with something. This is my thing." But I didn't truly feel that way. Once I started talking about it publicly, though, I realized what I had been saying (even if I didn't really believe it!) had been right all along. People everywhere are hurting. Some of the pain is minor and temporary, but some of it is major and continuous. Some is sporadic and unpredictable. Even though our experiences of pain are all different, they are all experiences of pain. And when we start to open up about ours, we allow other people to open up about theirs. That's so valuable, because talking about what's going on in our heads and hearts is therapeutic—even without a resolution.

I've also had the chance to share how I understand depression on a whole new level now. And even though our society is worlds ahead of where we were decades ago when it comes to being open about mental illnesses, unless it has touched their own lives in a personal way, many people don't know much about it or talk much about it. It's almost as though because we're not living in the joy we're supposed to experience when we are in Christ, we view admitting that we're dealing with depression as an indictment. But that's not fair, and it's not accurate.

If you're struggling with depression or you know somebody who is, please see a counselor and a medical doctor.

A Word on Suicide

Some of you may have read about my experience with depression and have been unable to relate, because what I'm going through is so mild compared to what you're going through. If your depression has been overwhelming, you may be wondering if life is worth living. Instead of glossing over it, I want to directly address suicide.

If you're considering suicide, whether it's something you're actively planning or something that has crossed your mind as an option if things don't improve, please reach out to somebody! You may feel like life isn't worth living or that nobody would care if you were gone. Those are lies. If you're struggling to find a reason to live, get in touch with a psychologist or psychiatrist as soon as possible. Reach out to family, friends, or spiritual mentors.

But don't stop there, because family, friends, and pastors are unlikely to be equipped to give you the help you need. Talking to somebody about it will be a huge step in the right direction, but the sooner you talk to somebody who is trained in suicide prevention, the better.

If nobody comes to mind for you to safely share your thoughts with, call the National Suicide Prevention Lifeline at 1-800-273-8255. Or use their live chat service at suicidepreventionlifeline.org to reach out to somebody. Don't believe the lie that your life isn't worth living.

Elijah and Depression

Elijah, in the face of difficulty (1 Kings 17), displayed some impressive fortitude and commitment to God, and he experienced depression almost right after. He went to be on his own immediately after God had showed up in a miraculous way. Even in the face of an unprecedented and undeniable win, he experienced doubt and depression and said he just wanted to die! I love how we get to see people experiencing an authentic, roller-coaster emotional journey in the Bible. Maybe we don't all know that moment of just wishing we would die because life is so hard, but we all know that feeling of wanting to give up on whatever we're doing because of the difficulty at hand or the difficulty that lies ahead. We know we're in good company when we see that same experience playing out in Elijah's life.

To set the stage for the story, we need a little background. King Omri was considered the most evil king Israel had ever seen when he took over and reigned in Israel. Scripture has nothing positive to say about him, despite his commercial success and that neighboring nations were still referring to Israel as "the land of Omri" over one hundred years after his death. Omri led Israel away from worshiping only God, and he was roundly criticized and viewed negatively by the author of 1 Kings. One big negative action he took was arranging for a politically genius marriage of alliance between his son Ahab and Jezebel of Phoenicia. After taking over for his father, King Ahab allowed Jezebel to introduce her foreign gods into daily life in Israel, and the legacy of Omri was solidified and even built upon—a legacy of drawing God's people away from God.

Try to imagine how hopeless and depressing this must have been for a true follower of God amid this religious change. The nation grew further and further from the Lord. And in that world we join Elijah in a well-known moment from his life, when he made a deal to settle the debate between the followers of Baal and the followers of God.

He proposed a contest to see which deity could intervene in the course of human events, pitting himself directly against the king and queen by setting up this challenge! He didn't just put God's reputation on the line; he also risked an unrecoverable alienation between him and his connection to the ultimate powers in Israel. That can be hard for us to conceptualize as Westerners. We see people do comedic impressions of our leaders and call them idiots for the ideas they're putting forward. We see people mock presidents and prime ministers openly, with few to no consequences. It wasn't like that in the ancient world. What the king or queen thought about you could easily be the difference between life and death.

Even though he knew defying the king and queen would cost him, Elijah set up a challenge between God and Baal and came up with the rules for the contest: the prophets of Baal would offer a sacrifice to Baal and he would offer a sacrifice to God. Whichever deity answered with fire from heaven would be declared the winner. Elijah had the prophets of Baal go first. They cried out to Baal, worshiped, and even cut themselves in deference to their deity. As the minutes turned into hours, there was no response. Elijah even started mocking them as they were yelling and, I would imagine, becoming more than a little desperate! After hours of nothing, it was Elijah's turn to prove that God truly hears and answers his prophets. But in a move of pure showmanship, he made sure they first dumped water on the top of the altar and the sacrifice. And not just a little bit of water; they soaked the altar and the sacrifice. *Soaked* it.

Elijah prayed,

> Lord, the God of Abraham, Isaac and Israel, let it be known today that you are God in Israel and that I am your servant and have done all these things at your command. Answer me, Lord, answer me, so these people will know that you, Lord, are God, and that you are turning their hearts back again.[36]

God answered from heaven with fire. Can you imagine how the adrenaline would have been shooting through the veins of anybody who experienced that moment? As many Old Testament stories do, this one ends with a slaughter that leaves the modern reader uncomfortable and confused.

I won't spend much time on it, but this violence needs to be addressed at least briefly. People have come to understand the violence so common in the Old Testament in several ways:

- Some argue God needed to establish his law and his legitimacy through works of strength where he showed his dominance.

- Some argue the God of the Old Testament and the God of the New Testament are two different beings. One is full of wrath and one is full of love.

- Some argue Israel was a picture of the church, and the extermination of people and anything else that took Israel further away from God shows how seriously we need to be taking sin today—not in terms of violence, but in how we actively cut out sin from our lives and churches.

- Some argue God never gave commands or license for destruction of enemy people, but that ancient people made them up as justification to hate and kill their enemies. God had no part of it.

- Some argue that God promised Abraham he'd bless the world through his descendants, so if Israel lost its identity as God's people, all humankind would lose its pathway to God.

From my perspective, all those arguments have issues, but they give us a starting point for the conversation. However we make sense of these passages, we pick up the story from here and move forward.

Right after Elijah was affirmed and God showed up in such an obvious way, Elijah found himself back in real life. Maybe on a whole new level it dawned on him that he had basically made himself an enemy of the state. Even though he'd had death threats from Ahab and Jezebel before this point, it seems it all hit home for him at once. He looked around and felt as though he was fighting against an empire on his own. He told God he was sick of being the only one left.

Even though it seems like a weird time for him to sink into such a low place, I almost find more comfort in that! I think this is because my own experience with the depression phase of this cycle wasn't circumstantial. I couldn't tie it directly to a change in anything I was going through, dealing with, or looking ahead to. Suddenly, without warning, it was just there. Maybe you can relate. Either way, Elijah quickly found himself in a depression that left him so drained and hopeless that he wanted to die. He called out to God, but it was in a "can we just get this over with" sort of way.

Again, this is an example from Scripture of a person who was used mightily by God as he was dealing with these stages of grief. If Moses and Elijah, the two people who appeared with Jesus at his transfiguration, handled these stages of grief immaturely and inappropriately, we're in good company. That's not an excuse as much as a reminder that we will hurt as we find ourselves in this hurting world. And when we're hurting, responding to that hurt in unhealthy ways is bound to happen.

The encouraging news is that God continued to use Elijah after this moment! Sometimes we can let the fact that we've experienced times—even years—of depression limit what we see as the potential for God to use us. He doesn't set such limits. We can mentally put an artificial ceiling on our lives because we don't think of ourselves as qualified enough or holy enough to be used by God. That's not what he's looking for. If he wanted qualified and holy people, he never would have used or called 95 percent (or more!) of the people he used all through Scripture.

Jesus and Depression

Jesus's experience with depression is probably best showcased by his response to looking out over Jerusalem, heartbroken because of their deep hurt and lost-ness. He knew the alienation and damage represented within his field of vision in that moment. He knew he had been traveling and teaching about the kingdom, and he knew firsthand the rejection and misunderstanding that had gone along with that. He knew people didn't have to live in such a disconnected way. But the incredible factor in how Jesus handled this heartbreak is that, although he allowed this reality to get to him, he also made sure it informed his actions.

> As he approached Jerusalem and saw the city, he wept over it and said, "If you, even you, had only known on this day what would bring you peace—but now it is hidden from your eyes. The days will come upon you when your enemies will build an embankment against you and encircle you and hem you in on every side. They will dash you to the ground, you and the children within your walls. They will not leave one stone on another, because you did not recognize the time of God's coming to you."[37]

He knew they were missing the whole point of why he came. The promise of the Messiah had come to be understood as the rise of a new, anointed leader of God, who would free the Jewish people and nation from the rule of conquering empires around them. The time between when the book of Nehemiah was written to the birth of Christ was around four hundred years. These years were rough for the people living in Israel and Judah. They were first conquered and ruled by the Persians. From the perspective of the conquered people, the Persians were a good ruling group. They allowed the Jewish people to continue to practice their own religion, and their thinking was that the more continuity they allowed their conquered nations, the more likely they were to keep from revolting or doing anything to shrug off their rule.

Alexander the Great conquered the Persians and brought Greek culture and language to the land. Again, this was a decent time for the subjugated Israelite people, but the polytheism of the Greeks began to make its way into the religious worldview of Israel. When Alexander the Great died young and unexpectedly, he did so without an heir or clear succession plan. His four top generals divided up the kingdom, basically the entire known world.

In this divided kingdom, eventually a guy named Antiochus rose to power. He gave himself the name Epiphanes, which meant "the visible god," the same root for the word *epiphany* we use today. Even though the Jewish people had been conquered already, this is where their situation essentially becomes a worst-case scenario. Antiochus Epiphanes did everything he could to denigrate and exterminate the Jewish people and their religion. He outlawed observing the Sabbath and practicing circumcision. He destroyed every copy of Scripture he could find and sold thousands of Jewish families into slavery. His ultimate insult was sacrificing a pig in the temple, which combined one of the dirtiest animals most offensive to a Jewish person with the most holy site in the Jewish faith. He wanted to hammer home the point that their God was unseen and powerless to stop him, "the visible god."

But it didn't stop there. Around sixty years before Jesus's birth, Rome conquered. They taxed and oppressed the people. And as we know from the story of the birth of Jesus, Herod started exterminating male babies to stop this "coming king" he had been told about from eventually rising to power. Religiously, the Pharisees and Sadducees took over. Pharisees were strict and one-upped God's laws at times. Sadducees were for the upper class and led the religion that way. Into this world Jesus was born, to a Jewish people who hadn't seen God move in hundreds of years. They had stories from the past to go on, but they hadn't experienced his work in their lives. They had every reason to believe the promises about a coming Messiah offered false hope. It would have been natural for them to feel as though they were destined to be a trophy passed around from conquering king to conquering king.

Jesus came to these hope-starved people, and he went to Jerusalem at the time of the Passover. In William Barclay's commentary on Matthew, he writes about a census taken thirty years later, showing that at least 2.5 million people were in Jerusalem for Passover, the huge gathering of the Jewish people at the most holy place in the world. "Jesus could not have chosen a more dramatic moment; it was into a city surging with people keyed up with religious expectations that he came."[38]

This was the backdrop for the "triumphal entry." If you understand the context and what the people meant when they acknowledged Jesus as the Messiah, you start to see why his response was to weep instead of to bask in the glory and recognition. He knew how deeply they misunderstood what he was all about. He was not the Messiah they were hoping he would be. He was much more, but they wouldn't understand that. He knew that, in just one week, once they realized he wouldn't fulfill their expectations, the cries of "Hosanna" (Save now!) and "Blessed is he who comes in the name of the Lord!"[39] would be replaced with "Crucify him!"[40]

However, even though he knew the road ahead of him, Jesus didn't let his deep discouragement and disappointment throw him off track. Right after he wept over Jerusalem because he knew how far they were from choosing to live in God's kingdom and how deeply they misunderstood what he was all about, he kept teaching and taking action. He went to the temple and drove away the money changers and those selling animals for sacrifices. And immediately after that, Luke 19:47 says, "Every day he was teaching at the temple." Although the leaders of the faith and local political communities wanted to get rid of him, they didn't because of how people were hanging on every word he taught.

I think that's the biggest lesson we learn from Jesus in the face of depression. He didn't shy away from the deep distress he was feeling, but he also didn't let that pain stop him from accomplishing what he knew he needed to do. That's the healthy pattern we see from him in each of these stages.

I want to add a quick but important clarification. There is a difference between the depression stage of grief and long-term, clinical depression. My words are not meant as encouragement to people dealing with clinical depression to "suck it up" or "power through it." If you think you might be clinically depressed, please see a psychologist, psychiatrist, or medical doctor. I've seen all three (as well as dieticians, exercise therapists, and a bunch of others) in my own journey through clinical depression.

But for those journeying through what can be identified as the depression of the stages of grief, we can learn a lot from the way Jesus handled what was happening.

Handling Depression Like Jesus Did

Acknowledge it.

We can't begin to deal with anything until we admit we have the problem in the first place. It can be scary to give depression a name because of everything we might attach to the idea of it. Just about everybody reading this will know of somebody who has attempted or committed suicide in a battle with depression. Many of us know of somebody who negatively became a different person in the process of being treated for depression with medication. But we'll be tempted to avoid labeling our emotional state as depression if we keep comparing ourselves to others or keep living in the past instead of dealing with our current reality. Admit it. After all, Jesus did.

Allow yourself to feel it.

After acknowledging we're in the stage of depression, we need to allow ourselves to feel it. In *Emotionally Healthy Spirituality*, Peter Scazzero writes, "Turning toward our pain is counterintuitive. But in fact, the heart of Christianity is that the way to life is through death, the pathway to resurrection is through crucifixion. Of course, it preaches easier than it lives."[41] What a refreshingly honest way to end a challenge like that! Even if we don't want it to be true, we find it is true when we allow ourselves to feel our pain and depression.

Allow yourself to express it.

Once you've allowed yourself to acknowledge and feel your depression, expressing it is the natural next step. In the passage quoting Jesus as he looked out over Jerusalem, we see he didn't shy away from expressing what he had allowed himself to acknowledge and feel. He was honest and free. A surprising amount of freedom comes from letting ourselves express what's going on inside. Whether you journal your thoughts, share them with a friend or counselor, or express them through art or something else that communicates who you are and how you're feeling, that expression is important.

Do what you can.

Jesus was continually action-oriented. Even when he was taking time to be alone with God, he was actively choosing what was most healthy. Even as he was facing heartbreak at knowing that he was being misunderstood as the Messiah, he didn't stop his ministry. He cleansed the temple and continued teaching in the synagogue. For many of us, the natural reaction—especially when our emotional state is being so thrown off—is to stop trying so hard. If we aren't sure of the outcome, it can be tempting to avoid getting too invested in going forward. Jesus modeled the importance of not responding that way.

CHAPTER 7

Acceptance

Pain, suffering, depression, and despair all put us in a place of brokenness and emptiness. As awful a place as that is, it's where we *must* be completely reliant upon God. And if we work with it instead of against it, an incredible amount of growth can result. Thomas Cahill writes this about the time the Jewish people spent in the wilderness between Egypt and the promised land:

> If God—the Real God, the One God—was to speak to human beings and if there was a possibility of their hearing him, it could happen only in a place stripped of all cultural reference points, where even nature…seemed absent. Only amid inhuman rock and dust could this fallible collection of human beings imagine becoming human in a new way. Only under a sun without pity, on a mountain devoid of life, could the living God break through the cultural filters that normally protect us from him.[42]

Depression brought me to the place of *finally* letting go—of my need for answers, my need to understand, my need for a solution, my need for a direction that would lead to an outcome.

Proverbs 16:3 says, "Commit to the Lord whatever you do, and he will establish your plans." The Hebrew language has significantly fewer words than English, so it's common for a Hebrew word to have two quite different meanings. Another meaning for the Hebrew word here for *commit* is "roll." That seems like a strange connection at first, but it makes more sense when you visualize the act of rolling something. Using this same word, Genesis 29:3 talks about rolling a stone. Rolling a large stone was one of the easiest ways for ancient people to manipulate their environment and use the stone as a base for whatever they were going to build. That's a strange visual for us, but it would've been relatable at the time.

If you have in mind this idea of rolling a stone, you're starting to get a fuller understanding of what it looks like to commit. It's the process of moving something, physically or metaphorically, from one place to another. In the case of committing, it's the process of moving something from a place where we try to control the outcome to where we acknowledge that only God has that ability. And then we give that thing over to him. We let go of what we've been holding on to so tightly. That's what committing something to God looks like.

Simple, but Difficult

I always knew I should be surrendering or committing my issues and worries and plans to God. And I knew that included my anxiety, frustration, and heartache about what I was dealing with health-wise. But that's so much easier said than done!

I can honestly say I'm finally at that point, and I want to share how I got there, because I never imagined it would be possible. I truly feel God guided me into a practice I desperately needed at just the right time: meditation. In the next section, I'll explain my personal practice of meditation, but I want to clarify that my approach is just one of many options people find helpful in connecting with God. As I've begun to share my personal experience with meditation, I've been shocked to learn how many people practice a similar discipline. They call it their time alone with God, listening time, quiet time, or one of a whole bunch of other names. If you're not familiar with this concept, it's distinct from time spent praying or reading the Bible. It's the practice of allowing God to speak to us by making ourselves available to hear him.

Giving God this daily time to rewire my brain has made a huge impact on my life, but I don't want you to think my way is the "right" way or the only way to spend time meditating or listening to God. Some people practice this time with God through journaling, some do it while in crowded places, some focus only on their breathing, and some do it during a long run or drive. An almost infinite number of ways exist to open yourself up to God, so focus less on *how* you do it and more on the fact *that* you do it in some way.

My Practice of Meditation

I know the word *meditation* might freak some of you out if you think it sounds merely "spiritual" and not necessarily Christian, but as Richard Foster writes in *Celebration of Discipline*, "It involves no hidden mysteries, no secret mantras, no mental gymnastics, no esoteric flights into the cosmic consciousness. The truth of the matter is that the great God of the universe, the Creator of all things desires our fellowship."[43] Meditation is our way of making ourselves available to God for that fellowship.

My first brush with meditation was seven or eight years ago, but it was just a one- or two-time attempt. My dad encourages both our family and our Winning At Home staff to practice the discipline of listening to God. I didn't really know what I was doing, but I wanted to try it. I made sure I didn't have any distractions by turning off music and light sources, and then I sat down on the floor in the lotus position and closed my eyes.

I hated it.

I had an awful experience. First, the lotus position is uncomfortable for somebody with bad posture! I was sitting there thinking about how hard the floor was and how tired my lower back was from arching it inward. On top of that, I spent those ten minutes with not much but negative thoughts in my mind. I thought of all the ways I could have done a better job with my responsibilities at work. I thought about what I'd done to hurt others and to damage my relationship with God. I thought about how what I needed to do in the future was daunting. I spent ten minutes feeling guilty and inadequate. After that experience, I decided listening/meditation wasn't for me. I didn't need that kind of guilt and negativity in my life.

Maybe some of you tried to practice the discipline of listening or meditation, had a similar experience, and wrote it off. I had written this practice off, but then I came across a book that gave me a new perspective. *Everything Belongs* by Father Richard Rohr, a Franciscan priest, is about coming to grips with accepting life as it is rather than trying to take back that control—which is impossible, as we all know from experience. But it sure doesn't stop us from trying! Father Rohr lays out a primer for meditation, and a few of the points he covers gave me enough inner momentum to try again.

The two specific points that gave me hope were (1) for the first ten to fifteen minutes, especially when you're starting out, you'll be bombarded with negative thoughts, guilt, and reminders of your own failures and inadequacies, and (2) a recommendation to use Psalm 46:10 to help guide the time of meditation:

Be still and know that I am God.

Be still and know that I am.

Be still and know.

Be still.

Be.

Armed with these two pieces of information, I decided I was going to try again. Because of my prior negative experience, however, I wanted to do a little more research first. I looked into how long I should meditate and how often. A recent study had shown that meditating for thirty minutes, six days a week, was the level at which the brain gained maximum benefits.[44] I'm generally an all-in kind of guy, so I decided then and there that I was going to set that as my goal and go for the maximum benefits. But please don't let that be a barrier to entry for you. If you can start with five minutes, or even two minutes, do it!

I didn't set many guidelines for what this time would look like. I only knew my phone needed to be in airplane mode so I wasn't distracted by a notification, I needed to have my eyes closed until the thirty-minute timer went off, and I needed to find a quiet spot in the house. That's all I planned when I started. And here's how it went:

Especially for the first week or so, I ran into the same negative thoughts of guilt and worry and inadequacy. But this time, I knew that was normal and I knew to expect it, which helped a ton! I found that once I got past those, it wasn't as hard to quiet my mind as I thought it would be. I just kept repeating Psalm 46:10 over and over in my mind. And then again. And then again.

Do you get what I'm saying? Thirty minutes felt like an unbelievably long time! I can't tell you how many days I sat there thinking something must've been wrong with the timer on my phone. There was no way it hadn't been thirty minutes yet; it felt like an hour *at least*! Eventually, that obsession with the timer would pass, and I'd get back into the sweet spot of just focusing on my breathing and the verse I was repeating as a centering thought.

During the first several weeks of practicing meditation, I never felt God used this time to reveal anything to me or to speak to me. But even then I realized how beneficial it was. Just taking that short break from everything else in my life brought a sense of peace unfamiliar to me. As I continue to practice meditation, on lots of days I'm doing it because it's a discipline, not because I feel like doing it. Even on those days, though, I begrudgingly acknowledge the benefits.

As I kept meditating, I realized thoughts popped into my head periodically—about messages I was working on, errands I needed to take care of, and so on. By the time the timer went off, those ideas were gone. It felt like when I'm lying in bed, drifting off to sleep, and then have an idea. I convince myself it's such a great idea that there's no way I'll forget it. But I always forget it. The same thing was happening during this meditation time.

Since my dad had been practicing his listening time for years and years, I asked him how he handled the ideas that popped into his mind. He recommended I keep a

Acceptance

pad of paper and a pen next to me while I meditated so I could write this stuff down and then let the thoughts go.

I know I'm giving almost too many details about how I journeyed into meditation, but I want you to see that it comes with growing pains and stumbles and falls along the way. If you decide to give it a chance, I don't want you to have any misconceptions about it being an easy and simple process, even though it seems like it should be. That thought messed with my head a little bit. I kept thinking, *I'm just sitting down with my eyes closed. How does this feel so hard and complicated?* I want you to see my process so you'll know it's a bit messier than you might think.

I started out with Post-it notes on the coffee table next to my couch or on the nightstand next to my bed. I wrote down random thoughts as they came to me, and then I went back to trying to empty my mind. It was probably about a month before I thought anything I wrote down was something God was showing me about myself.

During that meditation, I'd written down the name of somebody I needed to apologize to. To make matters worse, it was somebody I hadn't spoken to in at least four years. I wasn't even sure I had his current contact information. Naturally, I waited a few days before reaching out to him. I thought it through from every angle, but I couldn't come up with any way it wouldn't be awkward and terrible. For all I knew, he hadn't even thought about me for years. Yet I needed to remind him of how I'd treated him badly and then ask for forgiveness.

I dreaded that so much. Maybe a situation like this wouldn't feel like a big deal to you, but it was weighing on me more and more as time went by. This might feel like overkill to you, but it seemed to me that the Bible verses about "putting to death the old self" made a lot more sense because this experience felt strangely like a death. And in some ways, it was. That's what we see Jesus describing when he talked about denying ourselves, or about giving up our lives. He didn't use language that sounds good, and I think that was intentional. The process isn't fun!

Again, I think Richard Rohr has some great insight into this concept: "As a culture, we have to be taught the language of descent. That is the great language of religion. It teaches us to enter willingly, trustingly into the dark periods of life. These dark periods are good teachers."[45]

In those moments when we deny ourselves, when we give up our lives, when we enter willingly into the "death" of

Acceptance

no-questions-asked obedience, I believe we experience God in a whole new way.

After I reached out to this guy and we had a conversation, my spirit felt so much lighter. I felt freed from this burden I'd been carrying. I wondered if I'd put off doing any listening or meditation because I was subconsciously afraid of what I'd have to do to be obedient.

Richard Foster writes about this mentality as well:

> The history of religion is the story of an almost desperate scramble to have a king, a mediator, a priest, a pastor, a go-between. In this way, we do not need to go to God ourselves. Such an approach saves us from the need to change, for to be in the presence of God is to change.[46]

If you're going to practice meditation, establish a listening time, or make yourself open to God in some other way, get ready to go on a journey of denying yourself. That's where being in God's presence will ultimately lead.

After hearing how that first experience of denying myself brought freedom, you'd imagine the next hard conversation God laid on my heart would be easier, right? Unfortunately, I didn't find that to be the case. The second hard conversation I had with someone still felt like a death. Dying always feels like dying. It was letting something of myself be exposed and then having a frank conversation about it. And it sucked.

But again, on the other side of the conversation and the pain, there was a freedom and a light-ness of spirit I absolutely loved! In the first six months of daily meditation, I grew more in my relationship with God than in all the times of growth in my entire life combined. That's why I'm staying on this subject for so long and in such painstaking detail. God used this discipline to change my life. And I truly believe he will use it to change other lives as well. I'm just trying to get the word out that I failed and stumbled and fell into this avenue of grace, and I want to pass this discovery about meditation along to others who might be in the early stages of disillusionment and doubt.

However, I want to add this caveat. When I talk about what God is showing me through meditation, I feel the need to explain how. In the first six months I was writing my thoughts on scraps of paper or in a journal, God revealed four things to me. Three of them were about conversations I needed to have with people to make things right. One of them was a challenge about how I use my intellect and understanding of different subjects as a form of control.

The point I want to make is that I wrote down lots and lots of things in my journal that had no spiritual significance whatsoever. And I want to give you a sample of what I'm talking about because, again, my goal is to give you a realistic understanding of how this process has gone for me. I want you to stick with it, even if you run into some of the same roadblocks I have.

Here's a snapshot of what my journal looks like. I'm going to generalize what I wrote to help it make sense and to be more categorized by topic:

Plans with family
Basketball card / eBay stuff

Plans with family
Plans with friends

Errand to run
Sermon idea
Errand to run

Errand to run
Task to do at work

Basketball card / eBay stuff

Sermon idea
Send a thank-you note to somebody

Sermon idea

Ask Annaliese if I was too picky about something
Errand to run
Task to do at work

Task to do at work
Book to read
Place to visit
Errand to run

Home repair idea
Home repair idea
Home repair idea
Home repair idea
(I got really in the zone here, I guess)

A reminder to apologize to the person whose name I wrote down a few weeks ago!
Errand to run
Plans with family
Errand to run
Home décor idea
Home décor idea

Acceptance

> Buy Tesla stock *(I still haven't done this and I'm almost 100 percent sure I'll regret it!)*
> Home décor idea
> Basketball card / eBay stuff
> Plans with family

> Reminder not to look at my phone to check the time during meditation

I apologize for having you read that. But again, I want you to see that if you're writing down a bunch of meaningless stuff, that's okay. That's normal. Don't get discouraged and give up. I didn't cherry-pick the pages I copied above. I started on page one of the journal and gave you thirteen straight days of my entries. And on some days I didn't write anything, so this was everything I wrote down over the course of about a month.

I know I'm going into lots of detail about this, and I'm probably over-explaining, but I want to communicate the significance this practice has had in my life, and I want to try to remove any questions or obstacles that may be stopping you from giving it a shot. In the first couple of months that I practiced daily meditation, I felt myself going through the gradual process of letting go, accepting my reality, and being okay with it. That's not saying I'm at the spot where I wouldn't make a change even if

I could, but I am allowing myself to live in the moment and be okay with reality.

If you're anywhere on the spectrum of grief, or even if you're reading this book to try to understand a loved one and their journey, I can't recommend meditation highly enough. But remember, it's a discipline. And as with any discipline, you won't always feel like doing it. Some days you'll have to do it as an act of will. But as you keep doing it, I trust you'll want to continue because of the benefits and how God is using it to change your pattern of thinking.

That's the biggest thing I've seen personally. Not only has God helped me to be more open to how he chooses or doesn't choose to give me a solution to my health issue, but I also find myself looking at things from other people's perspectives much more quickly and being more gracious and slower to become frustrated. I'm naturally somewhat quiet, so most of the change for me has been on an internal level. But I can see how differently I react in the moment, and I'm significantly more open and interested in how my words and actions affect others.

I started with the practice of meditation I described in the previous pages, but I've tried some other options as well. If sitting and repeating a verse for thirty minutes doesn't connect with you, don't get discouraged. You can cultivate the discipline of meditation in lots of other ways. As I mentioned before, I've been shocked to learn how many people embrace some variation of this practice. I've talked to people who practice mindfulness meditation for ten minutes during the middle of the day, people who practice a listening time with eyes open and a notepad early in the morning, and people who use their daily commute to meditate.

We're all wired a little bit differently, so don't expect what works for me or somebody else to be the exact practice that will work for you! As I've been zeroing in on the most ideal meditation conditions for me, I've tried apps for guided meditation, walking meditation, an isolation tank (floating in body-temperature water in a light and soundproof pod), and being outside versus inside. Each of those approaches has its pros and cons from my perspective, and you'll probably find the same. Again, the important thing isn't *how* you do it; it's *that* you do it!

Paul and Acceptance

After talking about the unbelievable experiences and revelations he'd experienced when God worked in his life, Paul wrote this:

> Therefore, in order to keep me from becoming conceited, I was given a thorn in my flesh, a messenger of Satan, to torment me. Three times I pleaded with the Lord to take it away from me. But he said to me, "My grace is sufficient for you, for my power is made perfect in weakness." Therefore I will boast all the more gladly about my weaknesses, so that Christ's power may rest on me. That is why, for Christ's sake, I delight in weaknesses, in insults, in hardships, in persecutions, in difficulties. For when I am weak, then I am strong.[47]

If anybody had reason to feel overwhelmed by what many believe was a physical issue in addition to everything else he had to face, it would be Paul! In addition to being beaten, stoned, arrested, imprisoned, and shipwrecked, he had to deal with some unknown thorn in the flesh. Based on a couple of the comments he makes in his letters, people have speculated it was an issue related to his eyesight. But as all of us who live through seasons of pain and suffering know, knowing his exact ailment wouldn't help us gain much insight. Just knowing that he dealt with an unanswerable issue—despite crying out to God for healing—is the significant part of this story. This man, whom God clearly used powerfully and loved

Acceptance

deeply, dealt with a life-altering, painful situation that tormented him. We can all relate on some level.

We don't know what Scripture means when it says God "said" something to Paul in response to his cries for help and healing. Maybe he heard an audible voice, but it's just as easy to imagine God comforted Paul's spirit in the same way he most often comforts ours—by speaking through silence and Scripture.

But however Paul heard this message, I can tell you it would be really, really nice to audibly hear from God that his grace is enough to get us through whatever we're facing. I even tried to base my crying out to God on Paul's experience during some of the time I sought healing. I counted the times I cried actual tears as the times I was crying out. But that didn't bring resolution. Then I counted the times I cried tears while I was spending an extended time praying specifically for healing. But that didn't bring resolution.

When we're desperate, it's amazing what we can trick ourselves into thinking! When we've cried out and tried everything else, we still don't want to admit defeat. To some degree, that's our culture messing with our heads. I'm not advocating giving up and not working toward a solution, but an extended time of pursuing every new dead end reaches a point of denial rather than indicating a strength of spirit or character. I'm still going to try new treatment and diagnostic options when I find out about them, but I am no longer desperate enough to try every long-shot idea I come across. I've moved into acceptance.

To me, that's the lesson from Paul. He gave his all in pursuit of finding a solution, but he didn't let the stigma of "admitting defeat" keep him from accepting the reality of his situation and finding strength in God. As I've been through this process, I've become convinced that the advice to surrender or to find your strength in God will feel like a cliché to people who haven't gone through all these stages themselves. You don't arrive at acceptance and surrender until you've dealt with all the previous emotions and stages. It's a *process* toward acceptance, just like everything in life is a process. Psychologists Henry Cloud and John Townsend tell us, "There is nothing that you are presently doing that you did not have to learn. At one time the things you are now able to do were unfamiliar and frightening. This is the nature of life."[48]

Just as we do, Paul went through a grieving process with his ailment that eventually led to acceptance. That's the destination of this journey, but I believe if we try to rush it or skip steps along the way, we'll miss out on some of the hard-won truths we can learn as we let ourselves go through the stages of grief.

Jesus and Acceptance

Looking for one specific example of what acceptance looked like in Jesus's life is missing the point, because acceptance is what his whole life was built around. He often spoke candidly about how he would be gone from his disciples' presence soon. He didn't shy away from the fact that he had a long and painful road ahead of him. Even in the prayer in the garden we looked at in the bargaining chapter, he ended on a note of acceptance.

The way Jesus modeled acceptance was more of a lifestyle than a destination. And specifically for those of us for whom pain and grief is occurring over a long period of time, seeing how he lived out acceptance day after day after day is inspiring. He often talked about the fact that he was living his life as a form of surrender to God. In John 5:30, he said, "I seek not to please myself but him who sent me." And in the Lord's Prayer, he taught us to pray, "Your kingdom come, your will be done, on earth as it is in heaven."[49] He was communicating such a bigger idea than ours when we recite that prayer. In heaven, God's will is exactly what happens all day, every day. Whatever he desires is exactly what heaven is. Jesus taught his disciples to pray that God's will would happen on earth the same way his will happens in heaven.

Because of how our world is different now from how it was in Jesus's day, we don't fully understand the depth of the word *kingdom*. But a personal experience taught me what that word means. When I was in South Africa, we traveled to the neighboring country of Swaziland—officially the Kingdom of Swaziland. Before we went there, I thought that was an odd name. But once we walked into the immigration office, I realized why it was called a kingdom.

Americans are used to thinking of England when we think of kings and queens. We realize they're more like figureheads than absolute monarchs. But that wasn't the case in the Kingdom of Swaziland. It's been nearly ten years since I walked into that office, so I may have some of the details wrong, but this is what I remember: this immigration office was full of pictures of the king, and poems and quotes on the wall praised him instead of praising the beauty of the country. We later learned he celebrated his birthday every year by marrying a new teenaged bride. He currently has thirteen wives. That was my first real taste of what "kingdom" meant. I realized that in the Kingdom of Swaziland, what the king says, goes. You don't want to be on that guy's bad side.

Handling Acceptance Like Jesus Did

When we pray for God's kingdom to come to earth, we're praying for him to have absolute authority. That's the life Jesus modeled. Philippians 2:8 reminds us that "he humbled himself by becoming obedient to death—even death on a cross!" Jesus didn't just pray and ask God to have absolute authority; he lived his life as if God was the absolute authority! That's what surrender and acceptance look like. Our journeys won't be toward the same outcome Jesus's journey had, but they will require that sort of surrender and acceptance if we want to be faithful all along the way. That's what it looks like to deny ourselves, take up our cross, and follow him.

CHAPTER 8

Staying There

You already know this on an intellectual level, but it's worth pointing out: acceptance isn't a decision that magically means you aren't physically or emotionally affected or limited by something. It just means you've surrendered your need to control outcomes. I still live every day in a fog. I still have emotionally down days. I still have times when it's all I can do to make it through the day so I can get home and collapse. And depending on where your pain and suffering are coming from, you probably will too.

I wish I had better news, but the reality is that you've moved the goalposts when you arrive at acceptance. Beforehand, all you can imagine or hope for is to get *past* your pain. Acceptance teaches us to live *with* it. Not in a way that idealizes pain or teaches that the only way to "truly" experience life is through suffering, but in a way that continually reminds us we're focusing on the wrong thing if we choose to see only our own pain.

Living on the other side of surrender and acceptance offers a freedom I never imagined was possible. I thought only two outcomes were available to me: healing of some kind or resigning myself to always being miserable. Through acceptance, I've found the third way: allowing my suffering to reorient my priorities and goals in life. Staying in acceptance is a daily choice I must make, and sometimes it's almost a moment-by-moment choice.

Just as we can choose to ignore God's will and leading in other decisions we make—what we spend time thinking about, what we say to the people around us, and how we treat others and decide to act based on our own wants and needs—we can make that same choice in our journey with pain. We can try to take back control. We can un-surrender. It's not the healthy or wise option, but it's an option. Maybe it's the "grass is greener" idea played out on an emotional level. I'm not sure. But I do know from experience that I can easily try to grab back control in a moment of frustration or fear.

When the unknown future feels too overwhelming, the same temptations that have always called to us begin to look appealing again. We can be tempted to regress and lean on our rationality, our willpower, our sense of justice, our need to understand, our desire to lash out. We can, and probably will, do all these things at some point along the way, but hopefully we keep coming back to surrender.

Staying There

Hopefully we remember how we dealt with this temptation in the past and avoid traveling that path again.

If you find yourself trying to take back control and feel that frustration rising again, don't freak out. That's normal! In those moments, try to remember the big picture of your journey. Try to focus on where you started and compare that to where you are now. Remind yourself of the growth and maturity you've developed along the way. By keeping that in mind, you can refocus your energy on letting go.

I'm writing this encouragement from experience. The initial natural high of the new experience of acceptance and freedom I found in surrender lasted only about three months. It's so strange, because I know I don't want to go back to living life the way I was living it before, but it's so natural to fall back into those patterns.

I want to be clear about this. I don't want anybody to find themselves questioning whether acceptance "took" for them. If you're bouncing back and forth a little bit, that's normal. It's less of an indication that you're still not where you want to be than an indication that you're a human being who's still on a journey of growth. And even though we all want it to work a different way, life is a process of forward motion followed by regression, growth mixed in with backsliding, victories mixed in with losses. If you're feeling that way, welcome to life!

In *The Unwanted Gift of Grief*, Tim VanDuivendyk sums it up beautifully.

> Acceptance and healing are different. In acceptance one experiences the light again, but the anxieties, fears, and sadness are still profoundly present. They are still present but manageable. In acceptance, the sadness and depression lift considerably, yet at times they dance their way back into our path.[50]

That has been my experience, and I believe it will be yours as well. You won't always perfectly surrender. And even when you're still living in surrender, your emotions won't always line up with what's going on in your mind. Even as I've been experiencing the benefits of having accepted what's going on and surrendering my need to be in control, I find myself trying to jump back into the equation and try my hand at "fixing" things.

Just as any practice requires continued discipline to maintain positive outcomes, staying spiritually and emotionally healthy and surrendered requires the continued discipline of letting go and reminding yourself that God is in control. I'm not a good picture of maintaining discipline when it comes to being physically fit or staying at a healthy weight. As I said before, I tend to be an all-or-nothing kind of guy. I'll be extremely diligent about what I eat for six months at a time, and then I'll spend the next six months eating whatever I want, whenever I want. Or I'll get into a good routine of physical exercise for a prolonged period of time, and then I'll fall back into my time-tested pattern of skipping the gym or the pool.

As much as the physical disciplines don't stick long-term for me, it's easier for me to stay in the constant rhythm of discipline when it comes to practices for my emotional or spiritual health. Maybe that's because I see and value those benefits more clearly. I'm not sure. But for many of you, I'm guessing it's exactly the opposite. Much more clearly than I do, you see the benefits of being able to max out your bench press at 250 (and some of you are mocking me for thinking that's a high number), or run continuously for two hours (others of you are mocking me now), or fit into that favorite pair of pants (I keep two wardrobes so I don't have to buy new clothes when I go from 190 to 230 pounds).

I know these may seem like random examples, but I want to communicate the idea that we all have strengths and we all have blind spots when it comes to being disciplined. It's rare that you find somebody with equal focus and commitment dedicated to their mental, physical, spiritual, and emotional health. That's partly because it takes time and motivation to invest in health and long-term change.

If you've ever seen the stages of grief laid out in an image format, you're probably familiar with the U-shaped curve with denial, anger, and bargaining on the downward slide; depression at the bottom; and acceptance on the upward swing. I can't find the original creator of this image, but there's a hilarious version of that chart side by side with another U-shaped curve titled "My Experience" that just has squiggles drawn all over it and no coherent lines connecting one step to the next step.

That's more like what I've experienced. And moving forward, I'm sure it will continue to be my experience. It will most likely be yours, too, so don't get discouraged. Just keep surrendering and letting go of control. It's hard and it's scary, but it's worth it!

NOTES

1. C. S. Lewis, *The Problem of Pain*, reprint edition (London: Harper Collins Publishers, 2002), 91.

2. John Dominic Crossan, *The Power of Parable*, reprint edition (New York: Harper One, 2013), 252.

3. Timothy and Kathy Keller, *The Meaning of Marriage*, reprint edition (New York: Penguin Group, 2013), 60–61.

4. Thomas Cahill, *The Gifts of the Jews*, reprint edition (New York: Random House, Inc., 1999), 64.

5. Luke 23:34.

6. Junietta Baker McCall, DMin., *Bereavement Counseling* (Binghamton, NY: The Haworth Press, Inc., 2004), 48.

7. Carol Tavris and Elliot Aronson, *Mistakes Were Made (but not by me)*, (New York: Houghton Mifflin Harcourt Publishing Company, 2007), 70.

8. Crossan, *The Power of Parable*.

9. http://orbis.stanford.edu.

10. Nahum 3:19.

11. Jonah 3:4.

12. Jonah 3:9.

13. Jonah 4:2–3.

14. John 1:10–11.

15. Matthew 8:10.

16. Matthew 8:26; 14:31.

17. Marshall Rosenberg, PhD., *Nonviolent Communication*, reprint edition (Encinitas, CA: PuddleDancer Press, 2005), 144.

18. Numbers 20:10–11.

19. Numbers 20:12.

20. Mark 3:4–5.

21. Lewis, *The Problem of Pain*.

Notes

22. Frederick W. Schmidt Jr., *When Suffering Persists* (Harrisburg, PA: Morehouse Publishing, 2001), 93.

23. Tim P. VanDuivendyk, DMin., *The Unwanted Gift of Grief*, reprint edition (Binghamton, NY: The Haworth Press, Inc., 2006), 18.

24. Joseph Campbell, *The Hero with a Thousand Faces*, reprint edition (Novato, CA: New World Library, 2008), 125–26.

25. Philippians 4:12.

26. Deuteronomy 8:6–9.

27. Deuteronomy 8:10–14.

28. VanDuivendyk, *The Unwanted Gift of Grief*.

29. Genesis 12:1–4.

30. Genesis 15:3.

31. Genesis 15:4.

32. Genesis 16:2.

33. Matthew 26:39.

34. Douglas John Hall, *God and Human Suffering* (Minneapolis, MN: Augsburg Publishing House, 1986), 33.

35. Cahill, *The Gifts of the Jews*.

36. 1 Kings 18:36–37.

37. Luke 19:42–44.

38. William Barclay, *Commentary on Matthew, Volume 2*, revised edition (Philadelphia, PA: The Westminster Press, 1975), 238.

39. Matthew 21:9.

40. Matthew 27:22.

41. Peter Scazzero, *Emotionally Healthy Spirituality* (Nashville, TN: Thomas Nelson, Inc., 2006), 140.

42. Cahill, *The Gifts of the Jews*.

43. Richard Foster, *Celebration of Discipline*, reprint edition (New York: HarperOne, 1998), 17.

44. "MRI scans show that after an eight-week course of mindfulness practice, the brain's 'fight or

flight' center, the amygdala, appears to shrink. This primal region of the brain, associated with fear and emotion, is involved in the initiation of the body's response to stress." *Scientific American*, "What Does Mindfulness Do to Your Brain?"

45. Richard Rohr, *Everything Belongs*, revised edition (New York: The Crossroads Publishing Company, 2013), 45.

46. Foster, *Celebration of Discipline*.

47. 2 Corinthians 12:7–10.

48. Henry Cloud and John Townsend, *Boundaries* (Grand Rapids, MI: Zondervan, 1992), 265.

49. Matthew 6:10.

50. VanDuivendyk, *The Unwanted Gift of Grief*.